NORMANDIE
LINER OF LEGEND

CLIVE HARVEY

75 YEARS OF ENDEAV[OR]

This graph g[ives]
the length of t[...]
the loaded-d[...]
and the nor[...]

CROSSING THE ATLANTIC IN

12½ DAYS | 9½ DAYS | 9 DAYS | 8½ DAYS | 7½ DAYS

| 3554 TONS DISP. | 3300 H.P. | 5090 TONS DISP. | 5200 H.P. | 6500 TONS DISP. | 6600 H.P. | 7315 TONS DISP. | 9500 H.P. | 9160 TONS DISP. | 12000 H.P. |

| 1864 "WASHINGTON" | 1866 "PEREIRE" | 1883 "LA NORMANDIE" | 1885 "LA CHAMPAGNE" | 1891 "LA TOURAINE" |

UR AND PROGRESS

each ship :
tic crossing,
nt tonnage
se-power.

1900	1906	1912	1927	1935
"SAVOIE"	"LA PROVENCE"	"FRANCE"	"ILE-DE-FRANCE"	"NORMANDIE"
7 DAYS	7 DAYS	6 ½ DAYS	5 ¾ DAYS	4 ½ DAYS
22000 H.P.	14744 TONS. DISP. / 30000 H.P.	24838 TONS. DISP. / 40000 H.P.	44495 TONS. DISP. / 64000 H.P.	68836 TONS. DISP. / 160000 H.P.

"NORMANDIE"   "ILE-DE-FRANCE"

Cⁱᵉ Gᵉⁿ TRANSATLANTIQUE

"CHAMPLAIN".   "DE GRASSE".

First published 2001
Copyright © Clive Harvey, 2001

Tempus Publishing Limited
The Mill, Brimscombe Port,
Stroud, Gloucestershire, GL5 2QG

ISBN 0 7524 2139 5

Typesetting and origination by
Tempus Publishing Limited
Printed in Great Britain by
Midway Clark Printing, Wiltshire

CONTENTS

1	FRENCH LINE, THE EARLY YEARS	7
2	THE BIRTH OF NORMANDIE	15
3	TRANSATLANTIC MASTERPIECE	27
4	CROSSINGS AND CRUISING	47
5	TRAGEDY	73
6	IN NORMANDIE'S WAKE	89

BIBLIOGRAPHY	96
ACKNOWLEDGEMENTS	96

This book is dedicated to all the craftsmen and artists whose skill produced probably the most fabulous ocean liner the world will ever see.

Unrealistic, impractical, uneconomic and magnificent

The allure of *Normandie* continues long after her unfortunate demise – indeed, as time passes it appears to grow ever stronger as we are further and further removed from the more elegant age that created her. This book should not be looked upon as a definitive history but as another opportunity to be amazed by the courage of French Line to have built such a ship, to revel in the images of her luxury and to imagine the feel of that chill, smoke-laden wind that heralded her end.

ONE

FRENCH LINE, THE EARLY YEARS

NORMANDIE

Above: La Savoie, *at 11,000 tons, a transatlantic giant in 1900.*

Far Left: Transatlantic elegance, La Provence *begins another voyage.*

Left: The perfect culmination of CGT's first fifty years of operation – France.

On an icy cold day, 9 February 1942, while undergoing conversion into a troop ship, the former French Line flagship, *Normandie*, the most glamorous liner to ever sail the North Atlantic, was destroyed by fire and thus, a legend was born.

The origins of that legend stretch back as far as 1861, when on 25 August the Compagnie Generale Maritime was authorised by a decree of the Emperor Napoleon, to take the name of Compagnie Generale Transatlantique (CGT). In time this would become more commonly known as the French Line. The following year the company initiated sailings from St Nazaire to Mexico, the West Indies and to Central America, and by transhipment at Aspinwall (now Colon), to the South Pacific. However, it was not until 1864 that the company began operating a liner service to New York. On 15 June the liner *Washington*, proudly flying the CGT house flag, of a red globe on a white ground, from her forepeak, fired a salute and slipped from Le Havre harbour on that auspicious voyage. French Line were quick to establish themselves as the trans-Atlantic line of choice and, in response to the demand from both British and American passengers, calls at channel ports in England were introduced in 1876. It was in fact in that same year that CGT's *Amerique* entered service, the first electrically lighted steamer on the North Atlantic. In 1880 the Mediterranean Mail service was entrusted to French Line, which had opened an agency in Marseilles with an aim to develop traffic to North Africa. However, it was in 1895 that there was the first indication of the real glamour that was to become a French Line trademark. That year the company's 9,407gt liner, *La Touraine*, made the very first French Line cruise – sailing from New York to the Mediterranean, as far as Constantinople, and back. Not only was she renowned for her comfort and culinary excellence, she was also one of the largest and fastest liners of the day. In that same year CGT began advertising regular sailings, departing every Saturday throughout the year, from Le Havre to New York and vice versa.

Renewal of the lucrative Government mail contract created a demand for even larger and faster ships and in 1899 and 1900 the company took delivery of the 11,000gt sister ships, *La Lorraine* and *La Savoie*. Despite the growth of the company and its fine reputation it was a new, and more forward-thinking management that took over the running of CGT in 1904 and generated the impetus to build seventeen ships between 1905 and 1911. One of the most significant of these liners was the 13,700gt, *La Provence*. Completed in 1906 and capable of 23 knots, she was one of the fastest ships afloat and was able to make the voyage across the Atlantic in just six days. However, the CGT board was already considering a much larger ship – a ship that

France, *stylish and elegant.*

would be the perfect culmination of CGT's first fifty years of operation and an ultimate national symbol. Initially, it was planned that she would be named *La Picardie*. However, at her launching, on 20 September 1910, at the St Nazaire shipyard, it was revealed that those plans had been changed, and she took to the water as *France*.

France was CGT's first, and only, four funnelled liner and at 23,600gt she was really the first of what would become a spectacular succession of highly individual and very luxurious Atlantic liners for which the French Line became famous. Whilst being the

Lavish in her period décor; the First Class Smoking Room

...and the First Class Salon Mixte, aboard France.

largest of the company's liners, *France* was far from being the largest Atlantic liner afloat. At the time both Britain and Germany were building and planning ever larger and more ornate liners. The White Star Line's 45,324gt *Olympic* had entered service in 1911 and her larger sister ship, *Titanic*, was completed just a few days ahead of *France*. Meanwhile, an even larger sister vessel, conceived as *Gigantic* but launched as *Britannic*, was in the early stages of construction.

Across the North Sea the Hamburg Amerika Line were in the throes of planning and constructing a trio of massive liners, the 52,117gt *Imperator,* the 54,282gt *Vaterland* and the *Bismarck* at 56,551gt. Nevertheless, what the *France* might have lacked in size she made up for in her elegant and racy lines – when compared to the somewhat heavy and ponderous appearance of her competitors. She did not acquire the title of 'Chateau of the Atlantic' for nothing! Her lavish period décor made her one of the most luxurious liners of her time and she attracted the very cream of transatlantic society. *France* embarked on her maiden transatlantic voyage on 20 April 1912, just six days after the tragic loss of the *Titanic,* and this cast a pall over what would have otherwise been a glorious event. The elegance of the *France* and her high level of service and cuisine ensured her a loyal following, even in later years when she was being surpassed in style by newer ships, not only on the Atlantic but also on long and leisurely cruises. At these times her passenger capacity was limited to just a few hundred, ensuring her the ambience of a luxurious yacht – albeit a very large one.

The prestige and the glory of the French nation was all important and the French Government were anxious that they maintained their position, along with Britain and Germany, as operators of the 'super-liners' on that most prestigious of all ocean liner routes, the North Atlantic. Thus, a new mail and subsidy agreement was drawn up, one that called for four large liners and it was initially projected that they would be built over a four-year period. Construction had begun at the Penhoet, St Nazaire shipyard, in 1913 on the first of these ships, the 34,569gt *Paris*. Due to the outbreak of the war construction was halted. However, by 1916 there was an urgent need to use the slipway on which she rested for more essential ship construction work, so it was decided to launch the ship. The uncompleted liner survived the war, laid up in Quiberon, and was finally fitted out and made ready for service by June 1921. The whole ambitious plan by the French Line directors having been completely altered by the four years of conflict.

Paris entered service amid glowing press reports about her 'new generation' interiors. Gone were the gilded Louis XIV lounges and smoke rooms of the *France*, in their place were the sinuously elegant lines of the 'art nouveau style'. This break from tradition was the beginning of the creation of genuine ocean liner interiors. Public rooms that did not look as though they had been lifted from a Loire chateau, an English manor house or a Rhineland schloss. Sadly, these remarkable interiors would only survive for a mere eight years, for on 20 August 1929 *Paris* was almost totally destroyed while alongside at Le Havre. A fire broke out in her Third Class section, quickly spreading into Second Class and

Paris, *launched without ceremony during the war years, entered service in 1921.*

Her art nouveau interiors introduced a striking new look at sea.

finally engulfing the lavish First Class section of the ship. *Paris* was damaged to such an extent that at first it seemed very likely that she would have to be scrapped. Then CGT had second thoughts and she was sent to St Nazaire to be repaired and rebuilt. Remarkably, given the amount of damage, *Paris* emerged from the shipyard after just five months, not only repaired and restored but also modernised. The fire had given the company the opportunity to replace the by then rather dated 'art nouveau' style and now she presented a whole new look, one modelled on her fleet mate, *Île de France*. Throughout her career *Paris* was regarded as being one of the most beautiful and dignified liners ever to sail. *Île de France* had entered service, and surprised every traditionalist, in 1927 with a very modern internal look.

CGT had announced that *Île de France*, the first large liner designed and built after the First World War, would be the most magnificent liner on the North Atlantic. Their plan was to make her neither the fastest nor indeed the largest liner, and neither was her external appearance at all remarkable. With her three funnels, counter stern and flat fronted superstructure she was certainly a handsome ship but one not dissimilar to her older fleet mate, *Paris*. It was the revolutionary interior styling that excited her owners. The terms that were used to describe her public spaces were, 'boldly modern and trend setting' and after she had been opened for public inspection, shortly after her speed trials, the press were ecstatic in their praise of her luxury and novelty. Certainly her interiors were quite unlike anything else that had been seen aboard an ocean liner at that time. *Île de France* was a totally individual liner with a style of her own and she has been justifiably credited as being the pioneer of the 'ocean-liner style' of design. Her interior designers had taken their inspiration for her overall look from the Exhibition des Arts Decorative of 1925, the event that gave birth to the style that has become more generally known as 'art deco'. Therefore, both *Île de France* and the later rebuilt *Paris*, were the precursors to what would become the grandest ocean liner of all time, *Normandie*. However, at the time of *Île de France*'s entry into service, on 22 June 1927, the concept of *Normandie* was just a distant spark of an idea in the minds of the CGT directors and the naval architects at the Penhoet shipyard. As with the *France* and the *Paris*, the *Île de France*, with her air of *chic* attracted an enviable following, particularly of celebrities. Her remarkable First Class public rooms were often filled with European royalty and the Hollywood equivalent, politicians and industrialists and by 1935 she had carried more passengers in First Class than any other liner on the Atlantic.

Back in 1922 and 1924 CGT had taken delivery of two rather more modest liners, the *Cuba* and the *De Grasse*. Unlike the other major French Line vessels, they were both built in the United Kingdom. The Swan, Hunter & Wigham Richardson shipyard in Newcastle built the 11,337gt *Cuba* whilst Cammell Laird at

Birkenhead built the *De Grasse*. Strikes, material shortages and other complications resulted in the *De Grasse* actually being completed and fitted out at St Nazaire. At 17,707gt she was a far from spectacular liner and was not noted for lavish interiors or a passenger list of celebrities. The *De Grasse* did, however, find her niche and apart from her regular North Atlantic voyages and occasionally helping maintain the company's Caribbean service during the winter months, she became particularly popular as a cruise ship sailing both from New York to the Caribbean and from Le Havre to Scandinavia. By one of those curious twists of fate, this modest little liner would outlive her larger and much more famous fleet mates by many years serving other owners, and not actually being scrapped until 1962. The *Cuba* would not be so lucky. She had been built specifically for the CGT Caribbean service and was a ship of considerable elegance. Sadly she became a victim of war, being torpedoed in April 1945. In 1931 the *Cuba* was joined on the Caribbean service by what was CGT's most yacht-like of ships, *Colombie*. She was a mere 13,391gt but was nevertheless fitted out with all the style for which French Line ships were becoming noted. *Colombie*, like *De Grasse*, would also outlive the large 'glamour-ships' of the line.

In March 1930 CGT took delivery of the first of a pair of what were described as being 'cabin liners'. This meant that instead of carrying passengers in what might have otherwise been described as being First Class, this part of the ship was designated Cabin Class. (This was a fashion that would gain a degree of popularity for a time during the 1930s and the most notable liner to have her premium accommodation designated this way was Cunard's *Queen Mary*.)

The conventional profile of Île de France *contained a revolutionary interior.*

Lafayette, the first of French Line's 'cabin liners'.

The first of French Line's 'cabin liners' was the 25,178gt *Lafayette*. As a motor ship she had just one large and squat funnel and even though she was rather smaller than the splendid *Île de France* the ships had very similar profiles. Internally *Lafayette* followed the same design ethic as her larger fleet mate being furnished and decorated in art deco style. However, whereas on the *Île de France* it had been done in a rather eclectic combination, aboard the *Lafayette,* as befitted her 'cabin' status, it was simpler and rather more sleek. *Lafayette* proved herself to be a most popular ship both on the North Atlantic run and also as a cruise ship. Sadly, hers was to be a short-lived career. On 4 May 1938, while being overhauled at Le Havre, she caught fire and was completely destroyed.

The second 'cabin liner', *Champlain*, was launched on 15 August 1931 and completed in May the following year. She had a much more modern look about her than the *Lafayette*, with a gracefully flared bow, distinctively designed funnel with a slanted smoke deflecting top and with uncluttered upper decks. Her design was in many ways a herald of *Normandie*, which was by that time well into the design stages. Sadly, *Champlain* would always be in the shadow of *Normandie*. This was a great pity as *Champlain* was one of the most stylish-looking liners of the period and it has been said that she was one of the most smartly decorated liners of the thirties. Again the look was a version of the Art Deco style and both her Cabin Class Smoke Room and Grand Lounge were particularly richly panelled, and luxuriously decorated and furnished. On her Promenade

Deck was the two-deck high, Main Foyer, and very much as with the atria found aboard cruise ships seventy years later, this was used as an entertainment space. *Champlain*'s external appearance was further enhanced by having her already strikingly-designed funnel heightened after it was discovered that the original, lower design caused smoke and smuts to fall on her after decks. This enlarged and uniquely designed funnel also seemed to act as a herald of the impressive funnels that would become *Normandie*'s signature. *Champlain* was blessed with a marginally more successful life under the CGT banner than *Lafayette,* both on the Atlantic run and as a cruise ship. Her 28,184gt made her an ideal size to undertake cruising duties. Her role as a cruise ship took her as far a field as Scandinavia, West Africa and the Caribbean. It was unfortunate that this fine liner should become an early victim of the Second World War. She was lost in June 1940 after having struck a mine near La Pallice.

CGT were not alone, of course, in expanding their fleet of ocean liners during the 1920s but, despite having a fleet of very luxurious and popular vessels on the North Atlantic service, it was Britain's Cunard Line that was pre-eminent on the route, even though by the late 1920s their fleet was becoming somewhat dated. For example the prestigious accolade for the fastest transatlantic crossing, the Blue Riband, was still in the hands of their 1907-built *Mauretania*. Meanwhile, in Germany, the companies, North German Lloyd and Hamburg-Amerika had also built up impressive fleets of liners for their North Atlantic and other services. Germany's rise from the economic distress that had followed the First World War was remarkable and by 1926 they were ready once more to re-establish a premier German passenger service on the Atlantic. Plans were drawn up for two splendid liners that would restore Germany to the first league of prestige ocean liner operators. Their aim was undoubtedly to overcome the British supremacy, represented by Cunard, and to once again capture the Blue Riband. The two ships designed to place Germany in this pre-eminent position were named *Bremen* and *Europa* at launching ceremonies held on consecutive days in August 1928. The plan for the ships to depart on their maiden voyages for New York on the same day in 1929 was, however, thwarted by a fire that seriously delayed the fitting out of *Europa*. The fitting out of *Bremen* continued and she departed as scheduled, on 24 June, and took the Blue Riband away from the elderly *Mauretania*. Her average speed for the westbound crossing was 27.83 knots and on her return voyage it was 27.92 knots. *Europa* joined *Bremen* on the Atlantic in March 1930 and despite unfavourable weather managed to capture the Blue Riband from her sister. *Bremen* and *Europa* were

The stylish Champlain, *on her maiden arrival in New York.*

magnificent twins and presented very modern profiles, handsome and powerful. The face of the ocean liner was changing.

In August 1931 the Italian company, Navigazione Generale Italiana launched their new flagship, *Rex,* and the following month Lloyd Sabaudo launched the *Conte Di Savoia*. By the time these ships were ready to enter service, in September and November 1932, respectively, their owners had been absorbed into the newly formed Italia Flotte Riunite. *Rex* was 51,062gt and *Conte Di Savoia* was slightly smaller, at 48,502gt. Though far from identical they were two of the most beautiful and strikingly decorated Atlantic liners of the 1930s, the *Conte Di Savoia* having the more modern profile and interior styling and was more than a match for the likes of the *Île De France*. It was, however, *Rex* that would win the glory, for in August 1933 in a record crossing of the Atlantic, she grasped the fabled Blue Riband from the *Europa*.

At the same time that the directors of North German Lloyd had begun drawing up plans for *Bremen* and *Europa* the directors of Cunard Line had realised that they needed to invest in new tonnage and replace their ageing liners. Also, at this time White Star Line had begun planning the construction of a new liner. To be named *Oceanic* she would be the first liner of over 1,000ft in length, she would be a motor ship, powered by the largest diesel engines ever put into a ship and would be of 60,000gt. Her keel was laid at the Harland & Wolff shipyard in 1928 but, as the once prestigious company was in a dire financial situation, the work was soon abandoned. Cunard, however, had continued to work on the plans

13

for their large new liner and there seemed every indication that she would become the world's first 1,000ft long vessel. On 28 May 1930 the directors of Cunard Line informed the John Brown shipyard on Clydebank that they had won the contract to build the new Cunarder. The shipyard designated her Hull 534.

Shortly after the end of the First World War the French Government had recognised that since the drawing up of their earlier mail contract with CGT, the world had somewhat changed. The contract was therefore amended and it allowed the line to build two more ships rather than the three it had originally called for. The first ship was required by the terms of the contract to enter service by 1927, and ultimately became the *Île de France*. A second ship was scheduled to enter service no later than the summer of 1932 and there were those CGT officials who thought that the ship should be a further development of the *Île de France*, a little longer, perhaps a little wider but otherwise very similar. The associate managing director of CGT, Pierre de Malgavie, along with several others within the company, had other ideas. Their sights were set on something altogether more ambitious, a ship that was not just the equal to anything that Cunard, Italia or North German Lloyd might produce but a ship that would be far superior to any other, a ship faster and more beautiful than anything afloat. Convincing the rest of CGT's board of directors was a difficult task but in the end they agreed with de Malgavie, to build such a ship was the only way forward for CGT.

So, in those final years of the 1920s the principal shipping lines of Britain, Germany, Italy and France were all deeply involved in the development of super ships of state. Vessels that would be a showcase for each country's art and engineering achievements, ships that would truly fly the flag of each nation and if alongside that flag there also flew the legendary Blue Riband then that would just add to the lustre and prestige of the ship, the shipping line and her home country.

Thus against this backdrop of oceanic expansion *Normandie* was conceived and the race was on.

Île de France

Cunard's Hull 534 was to become the beautiful Queen Mary.

Normandie's *German competitors,* Europa *and* Bremen, *berthed together, c.1930.*

TWO

THE BIRTH OF NORMANDIE

July 1932, the steel framing of Normandie *was practically complete and the construction of the superstructure had begun.*

Having agreed to build the world's largest and fastest ocean liner CGT were faced with a very serious obstacle. The Penhoet shipyard at St Nazaire was unable to construct a ship of the size CGT envisaged without enlarging its biggest building berth and creating an entirely new drydock. The government, fully appreciating the prestige behind the planned liner, agreed a loan to enable work to begin immediately on the dry dock construction.

By early 1929 the French Admiralty's designs for the new ship were well advanced, based on specifications that had been drawn up by Penhoet's chief engineer. They indicated that she would have an overall length of 960ft, width of 105ft and with a 36ft draft. Dimensions that would make her a little larger than the German liners, *Bremen* and *Europa*. Then suddenly, CGT changed their minds stating that they wanted a considerably larger ship. It appears that they were concerned that competitors from other countries might eclipse their new liner in size even before she had entered service. (At this time the White Star Line had announced the planned dimensions of *Oceanic*, indicating that she would be 1,000ft in length.) So, new plans were drawn up and the naval architects began making model tests based on these drawings.

Meanwhile, CGT had been approached by Vladimir Yourkevitch, a Russian emigrant who was employed as an assembly-line worker at the Renault factory. Back in pre-revolution Russia he had been a naval architect at the Baltic shipyards in St Petersburg and between 1910 and 1917 he had designed eleven submarines for them. In 1912 the Baltic shipyard were asked to submit designs for a new class of 'super-dreadnought'. To be known as the 'Borodino class' they would be the largest, fastest and most powerful vessels of their type. Yourkevitch was instructed to design their hull shapes and in doing so produced a revolutionary, and very beautiful, form – graceful and curving and quite unlike the design of any naval vessel at the time. Yourkevitch was convinced that his design would help the ships cut through the water more easily, at either greater speed without an increase in horsepower or maintaining the designed speed with less horsepower and lower fuel consumption. This unconventional design was dismissed by the Russian Shipping Board, on the grounds that the ships would be too big around the middle and too pointed at the bow and stern ends. They were much happier with a more familiar design that had been produced by the Admiralty architects. Nevertheless, models were built of both designs and were tested in the experimental tanks at the naval base on the island of Kronstadt. The Yourkevitch-designed hull proved to be the most efficient, much to the annoyance of the Admiralty who then demanded further tests at a larger and more sophisticated tank, at Bremerhaven. Again the Yourkevitch hull proved to be the better design, and was accepted. At the end of 1912 construction began on the four vessels – each of them with a Yourkevitch designed hull – but due to the disruption caused by the Russian Revolution they were never completed. In 1919 Imperial Russia was in ruins and Vladimir Yourkevitch fled, first to Constantinople and then later to Paris, his days of designing beautiful ships for an Imperial naval power now long behind him.

Having read about CGT's plan to build a new liner Yourkevitch's curiosity was aroused. He imagined that his 'Yourkevitch hull' would by this time be in extensive use, after all its efficiency had been well proved in the testing tanks. He was somewhat shocked

Above: One of the motors being lifted aboard.

Below: The immense hull, almost ready for launching, dominates the shipyard.

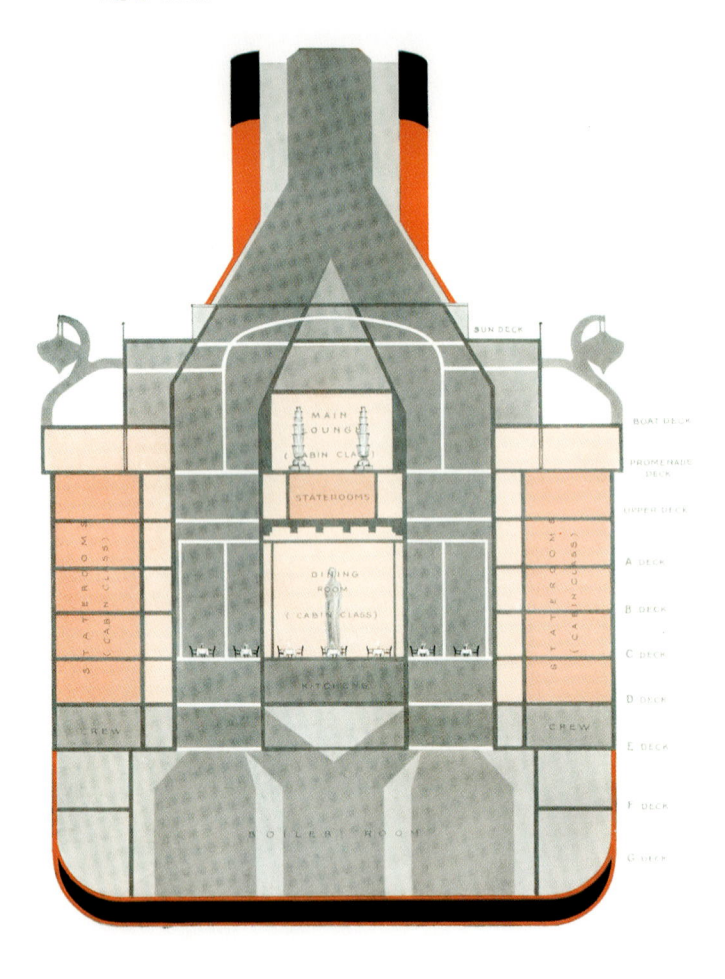

Normandie *in half – demonstrating her divided funnel uptakes.*

CGT by the French Admiralty. So, once again, Yourkevitch found himself competing against admiralty designers.

Despite Fould's misgivings the Penhoet engineers discovered that they liked the Yourkevitch designs, so he was summoned to the Penhoet headquarters. When he left he did so with details of CGT's required specifications for the new ship. It took him several months to come up with a hull design that he felt satisfied with. Yourkevitch estimated that a ship with a hull of his design would be able to make 30 knots with only 160,000hp and if his calculations were correct the design would save the company a fortune with its smaller engines and consequent lower fuel consumption. While Yourkevitch had been working on the hull design of the ship the staff and designers at both Penhoet and CGT had been at work on the other aspects, the number of cabins, the public rooms, the

to discover, when looking at photographs of the *Île de France* that nothing could be further from the truth. This most modern of liners actually had the hull form that his design had proved was inefficient all of sixteen years earlier. Inspired, he wrote to the Penhoet shipyard and explained his former role in pre-revolutionary Russia. His letter was ignored. He contacted them again but still there was no response. Then, with the help of an old friend, a former chief of staff of the Russian Black Sea fleet, who was now an Admiral in the French navy, Yourkevitch was able to get a meeting with the President of the Penhoet yard, Rene Fould. Fould accepted that Yourkevitch's ideas were impressive but in fact he was dubious that they would in reality be better than the designs drawn up for

Part of Normandie's *impressive turbo-electric power-plant.*

engines and the exterior spaces. Their brief had been 'to be as imaginative as possible, within the bounds of good taste.'

Following those instructions the naval architects came up with what was undoubtedly the world's first streamlined ocean liner. Covering the area of her foredeck that would be given over to the equipment and machinery related to mooring the ship; the capstans, winches, ropes and chains, was what was known as a 'whaleback'. This sweeping, shell-like structure would keep the waves off the foredeck and allow the ship to maintain a high speed even in a rough sea. Her forward superstructure would be a broad sweeping curve with her bridge wings following this same line. Perhaps where the architects had taken their design brief to its ultimate was with the design of the funnels. They would be huge, oval, raked at 10° in order to give an impression of speed and there would be three of them. The forward two would be functional and the third would be a dummy, to give the ship a more balanced look. However, it was not just there for aesthetic reasons, it would actually help distribute the wind pressure evenly over the length of the superstructure. Each one of the funnels would sit on a circular base in which would be housed the ventilating equipment. With this equipment so cleverly hidden and with a minimum of derricks and masts the ship would have clear and uncluttered decks and would therefore be able to provide her passengers with the delights of a full-size tennis court. The after deck would descend in six tiers and on the fifth tier down there would be a small outdoor swimming pool – at that time an unheard of facility aboard a ship built for the North Atlantic route. Then, with a final flourish they dispensed with what was at that time becoming very fashionable, the cruiser stern, and instead decided to give the ship a very beautiful spoon-shaped 'yacht' stern. Beauty and function went hand in hand as this design of stern was actually the best for housing a stern anchor, which CGT thought was essential.

If the new liner's external appearance was not revolutionary enough then certainly her power plant would be. CGT's engineers felt that, although propulsion by geared turbines had made enormous progress over the previous decade, experience gained in some steam ships tended to show that the reduction gears inseparable from this form of propulsion, in high power especially, were a

NORMANDIE

The sweeping lines of the Yourkevitch-designed hull.

Normandie's *original three-bladed propellers.*

source of noise and vibration. Geared turbines, while lighter and less bulky than turbo-electric drive, had an advantage, which could be set off only if very high-pressure, lightweight boilers were to be selected. Other technical reasons influenced their choice, but in general CGT decided that electricity was the more flexible power and that the total plant could be distributed over the bottom of the ship with greater consideration for the passengers than would be likely with geared turbines. This was a bold decision, as no Atlantic liner had ever been powered by turbo-electric propulsion before. However, it has been speculated that the choice was also another way of CGT saying; 'Look how new, how modern and advanced our liner is!' And why not? Nothing was to be gained from looking backwards, and as CGT were well aware, all the other major liners on the North Atlantic were as modern and as technically advanced as possible.

The French Admiralty architects had also been busy during this time refining their designs, and they had at last decided on the hull design that they would propose for the ship. CGT yet again called

An early impression, by Albert Sebille, of Normandie *at speed.*

for tests of this Admiralty design to be done alongside the Yourkevitch-designed hull. So, once more it was Yourkevitch up against the Admiralty, and as before, the Yourkevitch design outperformed the Admiralty one each time the test was run. Anxious to prove that their design was superior the Admiralty called for further tests and these had to be undertaken in Hamburg after the French tank was found to be leaking. Regardless of the location, or the variety of tests that were run, Yourkevitch's design continued to prove itself superior in every way. Nevertheless, the French design team held further discussions with the German technicians who had overseen the tests but the Germans were adamant, the hull form as designed by Yourkevitch was the superior one. Thus, faced with the inevitable competition from the new Cunard flagship that was about to begin construction, the directors decided to take the gamble. The hull of their largest and most prestigious liner would be based on a design that had never before been used on a ship that had actually entered service.

Just as these two great shipping lines were poised to begin construction of their largest transatlantic liners, the Wall Street Crash happened and with it the first symptoms of the Great Depression, that would have such devastating repercussions in both America and throughout Europe. American fortunes were lost in an instant in the crash and as a result the shipping lines saw their most lucrative market dwindle to a mere shadow of its former self. No longer were the wealthy Americans making their annual pilgrimage to spend the summer season in the glamorous cities and chic resorts of Europe. However, at this time French industrial output was on a high and there was very little unemployment. It seemed as though they would escape the economic disaster that had fallen upon so many other countries.

CGT saw no reason to delay the construction of their new flagship, and on 29 October 1930 they gave a firm order to the Societe des Chantiers et Ateliers de Saint-Nazaire-Penhoet, who in turn gave the project the code T6 BIS. The order was estimated at the time to be worth 700,000,000F. During the following three months the steel was delivered to the shipyard and the new building berth was completed, then, on 26 January 1931 the very first plates were laid down and the construction of T6 had begun. It was the very first stage of the race that would continue throughout the 1930s between the CGT flagship and her Cunard counterpart, as her construction had begun a few weeks earlier, in December 1930.

The designers of T6 aimed to make the ship as strong and yet as light as possible, ensuring her both the highest speed and best fuel economy. Her unique hull shape, being fuller amidships than most liners, simplified this task. Most of her weight was concentrated amidships with relatively little at each end. This would mean that she would experience less hull stress than her size and length might have lead one to believe. Also, her engineers specified the use of steel of a higher tensile strength than had ever been used in ocean liner construction before. Approximately 6,400 tons of this thinner, lighter steel was used on both layers of the liner's double bottom and on her Promenade and upper decks as well as in her main girders. This steel provided an equal amount of strength to heavier and thicker mild steel yet saved 900 tons in weight.

While the ship would, on completion, be a showcase for the glories of France she was nonetheless a product of international co-operation. For while her hull, designed by a Russian, was under construction in France, the Skoda Works in Prague were casting her steel rudder frame and shaft. Meanwhile, her boiler shells were being built by Press-u. Walzwerk, in Dusseldorf, her turbine blades were being cut in Sheffield and her propellers were being cast at Deptford, in South East London. Her lifeboat davits were under construction in Glasgow and the aluminium-frame bridge windows were being made in America.

The designers of the new French flagship took a further radical step when they decided to adopt the innovative design, first intro-

Normandie *nears completion.*

duced by the Hamburg Amerika liners, *Bismarck* and *Vaterland*, (and later also used in the German super-liners, *Bremen* and *Europa*) for dealing with the smoke and gases from the engine room. Instead of having huge up-takes running up through the centre of the ship and thereby compromising the grandeur of the public rooms, the up-takes would be divided and run up as close as possible to the sides of the ship, only joining together at the very base of each funnel.

By September 1931 the lower decks of T6 were in place and work was beginning on the shell plating. Every day an average of 1,500 workers per shift riveted another fifty-five tons of steel into position. However, the effect of the Depression was really beginning to be felt, with transatlantic passenger traffic down much further than had been anticipated. While Cunard were seriously worried and hoped the banks would provide them with the funds to continue construction of their new ship, CGT were confident that the security of being supported by the Government would insulate them against the worsening economic situation. The banks refused to help Cunard and despite an enormous outcry, work on the new Cunarder was brought to a halt that December. Across the channel it suddenly seemed that T6, with a large proportion of her shell-plating in place, would follow Cunard's 534 into potential oblivion. The subsidy for T6 was debated by the French Chamber of Deputies amid accusations that CGT had falsified its balance sheets, distributed false dividends and had altogether been involved in some questionable behaviour regarding its finances. The Minister of the Merchant Marine made an appeal to French pride, suggesting that France tell Great Britain that they would give up building T6 if Cunard would scrap 534. The patriotic outcry that he had expected against the suggestion never came. Instead a vote to continue with the subsidy was held and there were just ten votes more in favour of ending it. However, that night Premier Pierre Laval demanded that the finance committee revise the bill and vote again the following day. It was two days before Christmas, and it was the best Christmas present those workers at the Penhoet ship yard could have had, the Chamber of Deputies approved the revised subsidy bill, taking control of CGT out of private hands and turning it over to the government. So, St Nazaire would continue to resound to the continued cacophony of T6's construction, while the only sounds around the abandoned hull of 534 would be of rooks and seagulls.

During the summer of 1932 work had been completed on the distinctive whaleback that would protect the liner's deck machinery and forward superstructure from heavy seas. Inside the hull the workers were completing the basic steel walls of the public rooms and cabins. CGT had announced that she would be launched on 29 October and by the middle of that month T6 had

Previous page and above: two views of Normandie *being towed from her fitting out berth to the Joubert drydock.*

been under construction for twenty-one months. While she was still minus her superstructure and funnels her hull nevertheless had the look of being completed. In fact she was at about the half way stage of construction and was already looking impressive. On 18 October CGT had announced that the captain of the ship would be Rene Pugnet, formerly the captain of the liner, *Paris*. The following day, after many months of speculation, CGT announced T6's name. Everyone of course had their own ideas of what she should be called, from the inevitable: 'Napoleon', 'Jeanne d'Arc', 'Charlemagne' and 'La Marseillaise' to 'La Paix', 'La Patrie' and 'Victoire'. As always the names of those in the military and in politics figured large in people's choices: 'General Foch', 'Marechal Joffre', 'Clemenceau' and 'Petain'. Briefly, it had appeared likely that she would be named after Paul Doumer, the President of the French Republic, who had been assassinated earlier in the year. However, the day after the French newspapers had announced this as the chosen name the CGT officials having realised that there was little magic in naming their spectacular new liner after an uncharismatic dead politician, announced that all future French liners employed on the transatlantic service would be named after French provinces and that their new ship would be named, *Normandie*.

On 22 October the last of the scaffolding, that had surrounded T6 as she had grown up from those initial keel plates, were removed and the final work to prepare the launching ways for the big day progressed. Just four days before the launch there were only 153 oak blocks, supplemented by twenty-two large supporting sand blocks and fifty-eight smaller sand blocks, remaining in place beneath the hull. A platform, to accommodate the officials that would accompany Madame Lebrun, who was to perform the launching ceremony, had been erected at the foot of the great sweeping bow. Then, with just two days to go the weather changed and a howling wind whipped up angry waves in the mouth of the River Loire. The launching of a ship is both the most exciting and the most unstable moment of her career, so it would have been madness to have considered launching the liner under such conditions. However, not to launch her on 29 October would have meant a delay of six months, as there were only two days each year when the tides were at their highest, making the water in the Penhoet basin its deepest and therefore safest, for launching. So, despite the raging wind the work to make the launch ways ready continued. The early morning of 29 October 1932, launch day of T6, was cold, grey and still. The remaining sixty-nine oak blocks beneath the great hull were knocked clear and now it rested on just eighty bags of sand.

President and Madame Lebrun arrived from Paris on a special train and were met by the Penhoet and CGT officials. Once at the shipyard, along with 500 other guests, they attended a celebratory lunch and in one of the speeches President Lebrun referred to the ship as 'this super, floating cathedral'. Meanwhile nearly 200,000 people had descended on St Nazaire to witness T6 meeting her natural element. After the luncheon the Lebruns, accompanied by the great and the good from the shipyard and CGT, and preceeded by three priests and several choirboys, paraded around the launch ways with the vast bulk of T6 towering above them. One of the priests blessed the ship and the enterprise, and shortly afterwards thick dark clouds began rolling in and the wind began to pick up again. Andre See, chief hull engineer at the Penhoet yard, the man responsible for the launching, was suddenly aware that the launch could well be in jeopardy. There followed a hasty consultation with the official party and it was agreed not to wait for the optimum moment of high tide, not to run the risk of waiting and allowing the winds to pick up any further, but to launch the ship, and launch her while there was still a chance.

The timbers shoring up the hull were hammered out of the way, the eight cranes that lined either side of the hull were run up to the top of the ways, leaving the berth open and all but three large bags of sand were removed. The red, white and blue bunting around the launching platform and the large tricolour at T6's forepeak snapped in the strengthening breeze and the band played 'La Marseillaise'. Madam Lebrun stepped forward, grasped the magnum of champagne and swung it against the towering wall of steel; it shattered sending a foaming spray over the bulbous tip of the hull.

'I baptize thee *Normandie*' she cried and blew the ship a kiss. For a moment, once the hydraulic triggers underneath the hull had fallen from their slots, nothing happened then, the newly christened *Normandie* began to move. Some of the cheering crowd raced after the ship as she rushed towards the waters of the Loire, dragging four 25-ton piles of drag chains with her. They were there to help bring her to a halt so that the waiting tugs, whistling and hooting as the ship rushed to meet them, could take control of her. But the chains popped loose and *Normandie* was without their restraint, nevertheless, fate was on her side and the hull came to a halt exactly as planned, mid-river. At that moment the wave she had created upon entering the water came crashing ashore drenching those that had rushed to follow her progress.

Normandie was water borne but there would be a further two and a half years before she would be fully completed.

"THE SHIP OF THE FUTURE DESIGNED IN THE PRESENT"

	UPPER DECK	THEATRE	HALL	
WINTER GARDEN	A DECK	HAIRDRESSING AND MANICURE SALOONS	ELEVATORS	
CREW	HATCHWAY	CREW	B DECK	CHAPEL	HALL
		C DECK		
		D DECK	SWIMMING POOL	GYMNASIUM
	BAGGAGE ROOM			
GARAGE FOR MOTORCARS	FORWARD BOILER ROOM	MID FORWARD BOILER ROOM	MID AFT BOILER ROOM

THREE
TRANSATLANTIC MASTERPIECE

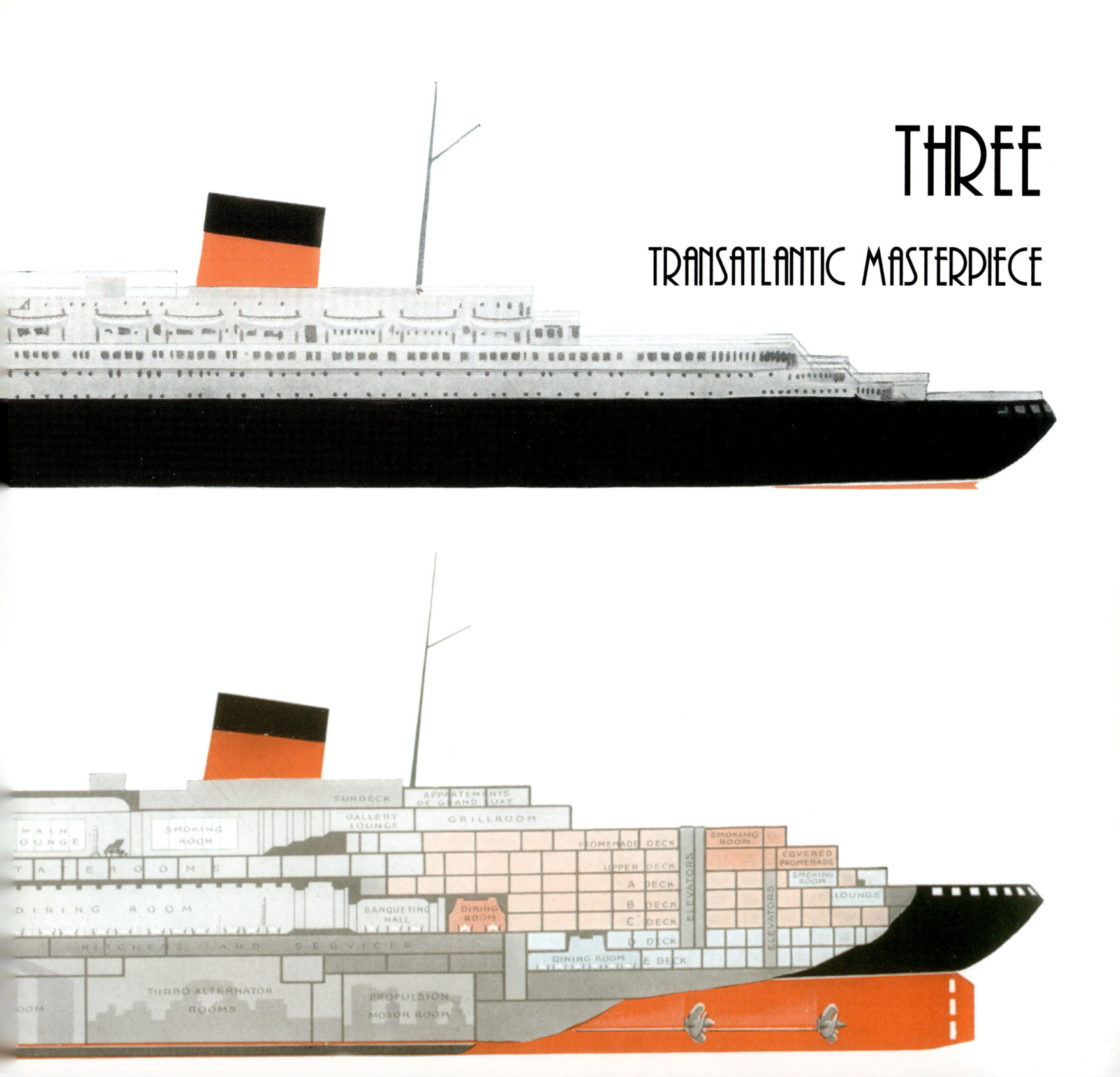

NORMANDIE

Safely afloat, tugs took charge of the newly christened *Normandie*, and guided her to the nearby fitting out berth.

As was to be expected, *Normandie*'s launching was celebrated throughout France. Even those newspapers whose political slant had required them to criticise her government-subsidised financing allowed themselves the luxury of revelling in their pride of this great achievement. Perhaps there was also some glee at having acquired the ultimate prestige of being the first nation to have built a 1,000ft liner, an achievement that Britain, as a great maritime nation, had been poised to call its own. However, the launching of *Normandie* did, ultimately, have a positive effect on the future of the rusting, partially built, Cunarder. Foreign competition was now the argument that the Cunard directors used as a lever to get a Government subsidy to allow them to complete the ship.

Whilst France was aglow with pride over their new ship, she was in reality little more than an empty steel shell waiting to be transformed into the world's most fabulous liner. Over 3,000 people were employed on the fitting out of *Normandie*, their task aided by three huge cranes.

First, the machinery that would propel this mighty vessel to her ultimate fame had to be installed. The power to achieve this was given to four main propulsion motors by four turbo-generators, each of 33,400kW output, a total of 133,600kW. There were also auxiliary generators, giving a load of 13,200kW for lighting, pumping, heating and so on – a total electric load of 146,800kW. (This was quoted in one of those comparison statistics, which were so popular at that time, as being appreciably more than the total peak-hour electric load taken by the whole of London's underground railway.) The generated current was conveyed to the four 40,000hp motors, each one of which was coupled to a propeller. The four propellers, which when cast, weighed 37tons each, transmitted a total propulsive force of 160,000hp, which was said to equal the horse-power of 100 of the most powerful locomotives. The power plant took its energy from twenty-nine main water-tube and four auxiliary 'Scotch' boilers, which had 3,500sq.ft heating surfaces, the former delivering steam at 400psi pressure and at a temperature of 350°C. These were arranged in special compartments forward of the main power room.

The power plant for the main and auxiliary purposes was divided into three portions – the boiler room, the main power-room and the motor room. This last also contained the distribution panel and high-tension switchgear as well as the refrigerating machinery and plant for conditioning the air in the dining saloons. The main boiler room contained the twenty-nine water-tube boilers. The main power-room was a magnificent two-decked space, thirty-six frame spaces in length. It was 'two-decked' in the sense that condensers, enormous circulating pumps and other auxiliary gear were arranged directly under the turbines which they served. Alternating current, at 5,000V was generated in four compound turbo-generators, and these were arranged at the aft end of the power-room, while above and abaft them was the main control panel for propulsion. This, so far as the space occupied by the switchboards was concerned, was a comparatively simple affair. It was only when the back regions of the board were studied that it was possible to realise the enormous problems involved in the design and arrangement of electric propulsion equipment for a ship of that size.

Facing the main control boards were two small boxes – two short levers moving in a fore-and-aft direction in each box were all that was

The pride of France.

required for manoeuvring each pair of 40,000shp 30,100kW, three-phase, synchronised propulsion motors. The main switchboard for direct current auxiliary purposes was at the forward, or boiler room, end of the main power-room, and this occupied practically the whole width of the ship between the inner bottom shell. This main board distributed the current from six direct current machines, each driven by a turbine through gearing, the turbines turning at 2,500rpm while the generators turned at 530rpm. These supplied current at 225V and were each of 2,200kW output. Some idea of the auxiliary requirements of the ship may be realised when one considers that the two refrigerating machines took 77.5kW each and the twenty special forced-draught fans took 57.5kW each and turned at 620rpm. For the hotel load there were no fewer than forty-four cables, and thirty-six cables for the auxiliary machinery. The steering gear itself, which was of electric-hydraulic type, had three motors of 48kW each. There was also an extensive emergency stand-by system on the Promenade Deck.

The entire propulsion machinery was contained in six watertight sections, four of which were devoted to the steam-producing plant, that is, to the boilers, the two others being allotted to the propelling and electrical plant. The maximum output, in continuous service, would be 160,000hp, equally divided between four shafts. It took over seven months for this mass of machinery to be installed, at the same time other electrical equipment was being fitted into place, in the kitchens, on the decks and elsewhere throughout the ship.

Between 1928 and 1933 several other very significant liners – P&O's *Viceroy of India*, *Strathnaver* and *Strathaird*, the Furness, Withy & Co. *Queen of Bermuda* and *Monarch of Bermuda*, Ward Line's *Morro Castle* and *Oriente*, the *President Hoover* and *President Coolidge* of Dollar Line, and the Panama-Pacific line trio; *California*, *Virginia* and

Left from top: With her lifeboats yet to be fitted, Normandie's *sweeping lines are accentuated.*

Finishing touches being made to the after decks.

Noted maritime artist, Albert Brenet, made many studies of Normandie – *these show her turbo-alternators…*

Below: …and her central security station.

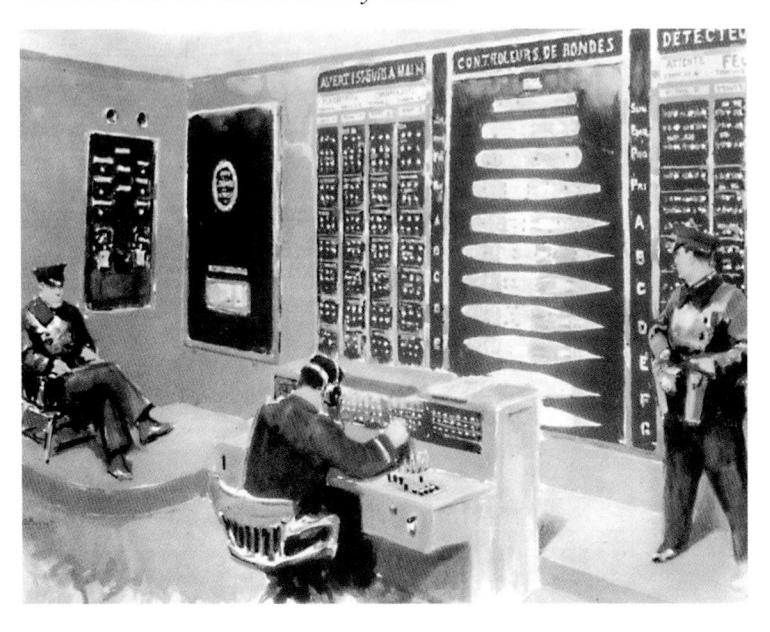

Pennsylvania – had entered service. Each one of them was powered by turbo-electric machinery. It is understood that CGT monitored the success of these liners closely and as *Normandie* neared completion her chief engineer actually made a trip aboard the *Viceroy of India* to 'get the feel' of a turbo-electric driven vessel.

On *Normandie*'s bridge was a new device, invented by a Parisian engineer, Maurice Punte, for detecting ships and icebergs up to four miles distant. This was done by means of radio waves that swept the horizon in 45° arcs, and when an obstacle was encountered it rebounded to a receiver, and an amplified beep could be heard in a telephone. Therefore *Normandie* laid claim to carrying the first rudimentary radar.

However, regardless of the frenzied activity in and around the liner, the new head of CGT, Marcel Olivier, made a devastating announcement. *Normandie*'s completion was to be delayed until the

Above: The Winter Garden with its flower beds and pergolas designed by Madame de Vilmorin.

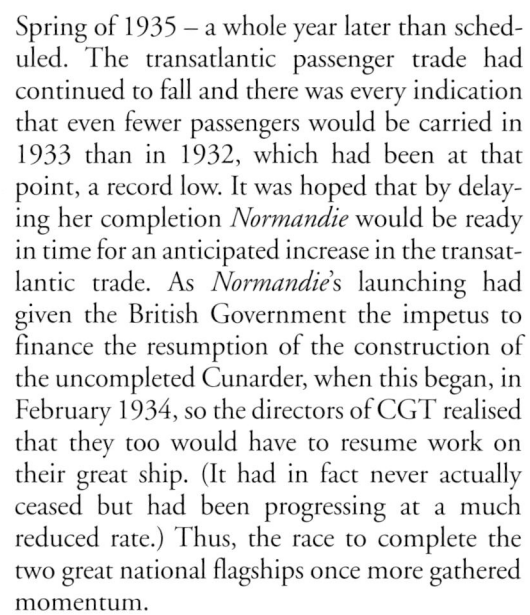

Right: The Upper Hall, leading to the Theatre.

Spring of 1935 – a whole year later than scheduled. The transatlantic passenger trade had continued to fall and there was every indication that even fewer passengers would be carried in 1933 than in 1932, which had been at that point, a record low. It was hoped that by delaying her completion *Normandie* would be ready in time for an anticipated increase in the transatlantic trade. As *Normandie*'s launching had given the British Government the impetus to finance the resumption of the construction of the uncompleted Cunarder, when this began, in February 1934, so the directors of CGT realised that they too would have to resume work on their great ship. (It had in fact never actually ceased but had been progressing at a much reduced rate.) Thus, the race to complete the two great national flagships once more gathered momentum.

During the early stages of *Normandie*'s construction French passenger shipping had been dealt two devastating blows, with the loss by fire of both the *Georges Philippar* and *L'Atlantique*. Therefore fire protection and fireproofing aboard *Normandie* was given the highest priority and the shipyard was determined that she should be as nearly as possible to a 100 per cent fireproof ship. Fireproof materials were used wherever possible and where other materials were used these were coated with fireproof paint and lined with asbestos. Also, using fireproof bulkheads, which were designed to withstand fire indefinitely, the ship was divided into four main fire zones and these were subdivided, by the decks, into thirty-six minor zones and then again into even smaller zones. Over 1,000 heat detectors were built into the passenger quarters along with 224 fire-alarm sirens. These were all wired into a central security station, on A Deck, next to the fire-brigade quarters, and incorporated a lighted display board that showed the entire ship, deck by deck. Also included in the ship were 504 fire hydrants that were connected to three sets of fire pumps, which had a total output of 300tons of water per hour.

As the work on installing *Normandie*'s machinery was nearing completion, so the work began on transforming the bare steel spaces into the elegant salons and luxurious cabins that would make *Normandie* into the ultimate 'ship of state'. It was the intention of the French government that she should truly represent France and in effect be the finest showcase of the arts, crafts and sciences of France. Earlier CGT liners, *Paris, Île de France, Lafayette* and *Champlain* had already been decorated in the art deco style and prestigious liners of other nations, such as Italy's *Conte Di Savoia*, and the *Bremen* and *Europa* of Germany, had also adopted this sleekly elegant look that was so well suited to the ocean liner. Nevertheless, while these and other liners all interpreted the style very well it was aboard *Normandie* that Art Deco and the 'ocean liner style' would evolve to such dramatic effect. This was undoubtedly due, in no small part, to the immense scale of her public rooms.

Above: The Gallery Lounge.

Left: The three-deck high Main Entrance Hall.

Yourkevitch, and the naval architects, having tackled the problem of the huge engine room uptakes, (which would have taken up so much valuable central space through her public rooms), gave the ship a vast central area in which her designers could create a magnificent array of flowing public spaces, which would ultimately be the largest public rooms ever seen aboard a ship at that time.

No single interior designer was given the responsibility for the overall look of *Normandie*'s public rooms and cabins. Instead, the list of designers that contributed to her interiors reads like a lexicon of the most influential exponents of the Art Deco style: Jean Dunand, Pierre Patout, F. DeJean, Jean and Joel Martel, Raymond Subes, Leon Baudry and Emile-Jacques Ruhlmann.

At an immense 79,283tons and an unprecedented 1,029ft in length *Normandie* could have been considered to be virtually just a First Class liner with more than seventy-five per cent of the ship being devoted to this class – 864 of her total 1,972 passenger berths were in First Class cabins and De Luxe suites. Those eight hundred or so privileged souls embarked the ship at A Deck, and a short flight of stairs took them up to the breathtaking, three-deck high entrance hall, its walls clad in Algerian onyx and enhanced with strips of hammered glass and gilded bronze that had been wrought by Raymond Subes. The two pairs of lifts that served this area were also encased in gilded bronze designed by Subes. Like all the lifts in the First Class section of the ship, in true French Line style they were served by two attendants in each – one to ask which deck the passenger required and the other to press the appropriate button.

The principal public rooms in First Class were the Winter Garden and the Reading and Writing Rooms, the Theatre, the Gallery-Lounge, the Grand Lounge, the Smoking Room, the Café-Grill and the Dining Room. Like the majority of the First Class public rooms, the Winter Garden was on Promenade Deck, and its forward location gave it a commanding view over the bow of the ship. However, the view, from its impressive sweep of twenty-eight windows was somewhat overshadowed by the room itself, as a French Line brochure would describe:

> ... the fascinating Winter Garden, well forward on the Promenade Deck, and looking straight ahead over the bow. It is a true garden, which sails the high seas in summer and winter, with pergolas of roses, growing plants and trees, glass enclosed aviaries of songbirds and birds of bright plumage, and a softly splashing fountain.

The Reading Room and the Writing Room were aft of the Winter Garden, on the port and starboard respectively.

Moving aft on Promenade Deck, the next major public space was the Theatre. Seating 400 people, it was fitted with a well-equipped stage – and dressing rooms – that enabled plays, concerts and lectures to be featured, as well as having the facility to screen films. It was a facility far in advance of any theatre aboard other liners of the time. (Even the new Cunard liner then under con-

Above and previous page: The sumptuous Grand Lounge.

Above right: The Smoking Room; the grand staircase leading to the Café-Grill,

Right: ...and the golden lacquered panels created by Jean Dunand.

struction would not be able to boast such a refinement, and even when a cinema was created aboard her after the war it was an undistinguished space adapted from a former lounge.)

Aft of *Normandie*'s theatre was the Gallery-Lounge. This was a vast space, luxuriously furnished and, above four alcoves containing semi-circular sofas, were bas-relief panels depicting a somewhat curious mix of themes: Commerce, Art, Fishing and Animal Husbandry. The main decorative features of the Gallery-Lounge were two huge paintings by Ducos de la Haille: The Conquest of Normandy and Norman Peace. The room was further enhanced by eight lacquered columns, four each side, supporting alabaster lamp-vases, which helped generate the impression that this was the grandest of entrances leading to *Normandie*'s most opulent of rooms, The Grand Lounge.

The Grand Lounge was two and a half decks high and was flanked by five windows on each side, which opened onto the Promenade Deck. This sumptuous salon has often been compared to the famed Hall of Mirrors in the Palace of Versailles, and justifiably so. Its walls were covered in four glass relief panels designed by Dupas, which were etched and painted on the reverse side using gold, silver, platinum and palladium. Each of the panels were 21ft high and 49ft wide and each one depicted a different theme: The Chariot of Poseidon, The Chariot of Thetis, The Rape of Europa and The Birth of Aphrodite. The principal source of lighting in the room was contained within four elaborate, 12ft high, towers of Lalique glass, resembling fountains, the base of which was a circular settee. The room also contained two massive pewter urns, also with circular settee bases, one forward and one aft. An Aubusson carpet, with a design of a basket of flowers, and reputed to have been the largest hand-woven carpet ever made, covered the central dance floor during the day. Aubusson tapestry, in grey and red, with designs of flowers also covered the modern-styled, gilded, chairs and sofas. The whole effect was both striking and luxurious. In their publicity material French Line stated:

> *This great, spacious room epitomises all the grandeur and simple luxury of the smartest French taste. Ships of all seas, since time began, are effectively pictured in the decorations and the very spirit of navigation is reflected in lacquer and glass. Splendid tapestries and floor coverings, weaving a romantic pattern of man's conquests, form a stunning background for those to whom fine surroundings and a gracious atmosphere are important.*

Above: The intimate 'Private Bar'.

Left: The most chic of Normandie's *public rooms, the Café-Grill.*

Overleaf: Normandie's *remarkable dining room.*

NORMANDIE

LINER OF LEGEND

NORMANDIE

Above: The Chapel.

Top: An early impression of the Café-Grill. Note the elaborate statue that would have dominated the deck.

Left: The Reading Room.

A sliding door, with a design of Aurora's Chariot, lead from the striking, glass-clad, Grand Lounge, into the rich golden glow of the Smoking Room. Jean Dunand created the four golden lacquered panels that clad the walls of this equally impressive room. Each one of the panels was 20sq.ft and, as with other decorations throughout the ship, each one depicted a different theme. In the case of the Smoking Room it was Fishing, Horse Taming, Harvesting and Sports, and Dunand had to develop new techniques in order to achieve the required colours and textures of the images on these panels. The room was furnished with brown leather armchairs, which were arranged around gaming tables. Aft, in the centre of the room, rose a grand staircase at the top of which stood a gilded statue, of *La Normandie*. It was, from the base of this statue that one could see the full impact of the public rooms that had been made possible by the divided funnel up-takes. The doors between each of these vast salons could all be opened up to allow a 690ft-long vista of Art Deco richness and luxury, stretching down that staircase and all the way through and into the theatre. Never before had there been such a suite of public rooms created aboard a liner.

That staircase took one up to Boat Deck to what was perhaps the most chic of *Normandie*'s public rooms, the Café-Grill. It was an oval room with a vast sweep of fourteen windows; in fact they were so large as to make it appear that the wall was made entirely of glass. Whereas the other First Class public areas were decorated in the Jacques Rulhman inspired style of Art Deco; with luxurious materials, rich fabrics, precious inlays and glistening lacquer, the Café-Grill showed the other face of Art Deco – Bauhaus. It was furnished with sleek, chrome-framed leather-upholstered chairs set around matching chrome-framed square tables. There were, however, touches of opulence in the form of walls sheathed in pigskin and lighting columns similar to those in the Grand Lounge. French Line publicity material described it thus:

> *The Grill Room on the Boat Deck is a pleasantly sunny room by day, while at night it is softly illuminated by shafts of iridescent light. It has often been called the* Normandie's *nightclub, for here refreshments may be had and there is music and dancing throughout the evening.*

While there is no doubt that by night it was probably the most glamorous nightclub at sea, by day the focus of the room lay beyond that great sweep of windows, rather than the dance floor. Beyond those windows lay the First Class Sun Deck, which had been laid out with a clever arrangement of zigzag screens and seating, to protect the passengers from the Atlantic breezes. It was

The First Class swimming pool.

NORMANDIE

Left: The Trouville Suite.

Below right: The Rouen Suite.

floodlit by night with large lamps, and the plan was to have the whole deck dominated by a truly fabulous statue, a fishtailed marine god with up-raised arms holding a trident in one hand and an elaborate seashell in the other. Once in place, it was discovered that the creation was both heavy and was affected so much by the vibration that far aft in the liner that it was removed even before the ship sailed on a commercial voyage.

The *chic* simplicity of the Café-Grill was countered by *Normandie*'s remarkable dining room. In their publicity material, French Line referred to it as *The Great Dining Room* and described it as being:

> In thorough keeping with the splendour of the Normandie's artistic mood, …rising through three decks, where Normandy landscapes in bas-relief, modelled in gold against red marble and with walls of sculptured glass, columns of indirect light and ceilings of gold, pattern a background of elegance and makes a brilliant setting for the renowned service and cuisine of French Line.

The room was a remarkable 282ft in length and provided seating for 700 diners at 150 tables. The passengers entered the room down a grand staircase that fully justified the term *grande descente*. The lighting was achieved by the use of thirty-eight monumental luminous glass sconces, almost 16ft tall, and by twelve light-towers of Lalique glass. These resembled fountains of light, which illuminated the ceiling. Standing over 13ft above the Captain's table was a bronze statue of a female figure, by Dejean, 'Peaceful Normandy'. Behind the statue was a smaller, though no less elegant, space – the Banquet Room, and opening off the dining room were eight further private dining rooms.

Down on D Deck, the deck below the Grand Dining Room, was the First Class swimming pool. This, as with all the other First Class facilities, was immense. In fact at 75ft long and 19ft wide, it was the largest swimming pool ever created on a ship. The arrangement of the pool was in a graduated sequence of depths, each marked by rubber posts. Completely encircling the tiled walkway around the pool was a 16ft high frieze, of Sevres tiles, depicting animal themes. French Line called it 'gaily environed' and suggested: 'After a splashing swim, it is a treat to sit at the unique gilded-bronze circular bar at the far end of the pool. The entire atmosphere suggests all the salt-sea zest of the famed beaches of France.'

There were several other, smaller, public rooms as well as an exquisitely decorated chapel. It was designed for both Catholic and Protestant worship and was described by the company as being, 'a cathedral in miniature.'

There were 448 First Class cabins and they were provided with full bathrooms or a shower and a lavatory or just a lavatory. The outside cabins (there were in fact only 126 inside) had two portholes each and these were of an entirely new design, hinging outwards to permit escape to either the boats, or the sea, in the event of an emergency.

The First Class passenger cabins and suites were every bit as luxurious and opulently decorated as the public rooms. The most lavish of *Normandie*'s accommodations, Suites de Grand Luxe, were located towards the after end of Sun Deck and were known as the Deauville and Trouville Suites. Each of these remarkable apartments had four bedrooms, a living room, dining room and five bathrooms as well as a servant's room and pantry and a private, 45ft, promenade deck, with an uninterrupted view over the stern of the ship. Adjoining each suite was a further two-room suite, for the use of additional private staff. The principal rooms of each suite followed the curve of the aft superstructure of the ship, thereby creating oval-shaped rooms. Folding black enamelled doors, inlaid with a design of garlands of

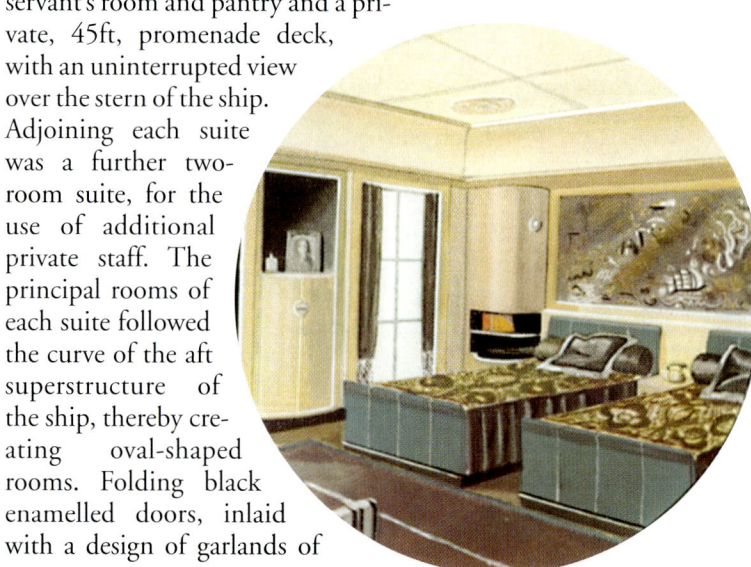

Left: The Deauville Suite.

Below left: The Trouville Suite, salon.

Below: The Rouen Suite, salon and dining room.

flowers led to the dining room of the Trouville Suite, which was lined with ivory leather and furnished with chairs in vivid green hide. The living room was hung with Aubusson tapestries and furnished with chairs upholstered in bronze-coloured satin. The Deauville Suite, while of identical layout had an entirely different decorative style, principally in shades of rose, beige and blue and with ivory lacquered furniture. It was described as being 'blond and gay, and extremely well arranged.' There were two other Suites de Grand Luxe, the Caen and the Rouen, which were located on Main Deck, which were equally as lavish but lacked the private expanse of terrace.

There were also ten Suites de Luxe, each one of them named after either a Normandy town or city: 'Alencon', 'Bayeux', 'Coutances', 'Dieppe', 'Fecamp', 'Lisieux', 'Mont St Michel', 'Honfleur', 'Jumieges' and 'Le Havre' (all, with the exception of one, were furnished and decorated in the most luxurious of Art Deco style, and no two were alike. The exception was the Bayeux apartment, which was decorated in the Louis XV style.) There were twenty-four special cabins, each with a private veranda, 16ft by 12ft. Each, too, had its own special scheme of decoration. There were, of course, more standard, but equally as beautifully appointed, staterooms. In their publicity material French Line said: 'Call it a stateroom or a ship's cabin if you will, but it is just a delightful little home if you happen to be a passenger on board *Normandie*!'

The Tourist Class passengers had accommodation extending over three decks, with an array of stylish, though somewhat less lavish, public rooms. The Dining Room was particularly elegant. Its centre section was dominated by five great glass columns that supported an illuminated dome that extended up through two decks. The Tourist Class lounge was every bit the equal to First Class in other liners. It was a very pretty room, panelled in white sycamore, and furnished with chairs covered in Aubusson tapestry with the same floral design as those in the First Class lounge. Those travelling in Tourist Class also had the unique facility of the open-air swimming pool, located aft on Main Deck. For a liner employed on the northerly route across the Atlantic this was a somewhat curious addition and actually had the look of being rather an after thought, stuck out in its rather exposed position. Also it seemed curious to provide such a facility and yet not provide any sheltered lido area. The whole of the accommodation for Third Class passengers was situated aft instead of forward, as was often the case in large liners at the time. There was a large sheltered sun deck for this class as well as an open promenade, smoking room, bar, lounge and dining room. According to a report at the time: 'The crew's quarters are fitted out to a high standard and are reminiscent of the Second Class in older ships.'

Above: The Dieppe Suite.

Above left: The Jumieges Suite.

Top right:: A cabin with a terrace.

Centre right: An outside cabin.

Bottom right: An inside cabin.

When the *Champlain* had been introduced into French Line service in 1932 her open deck space was almost radical in that it was relatively clear of machinery. *Normandie*'s designers took this concept even further and her decks were absolutely stripped of ventilators, air fans, winches and other details. Her ventilating system was concealed in the superstructure and was operated by means of fans; the whole of the navigating equipment – windlasses, winches and the like – were arranged underneath the turtleback. This arrangement gave a large clear area suitable for deck sports, which then was beginning to be seen as an important facility, even aboard a transatlantic liner. Aft, the various decks ended in successively receding stages, beginning with the Promenade Deck and finishing at A Deck, the whole forming terraces where passengers of all classes had a clear view of the sea. Of the three enormous funnels, the after, dummy one, contained a series of dog kennels. The funnels were streamlined, their height decreasing from forward to aft, and they were slanted at 10°. The two forward funnels were specially designed to prevent any boiler deposits from falling onto the deck. The two pole masts were also raked, but at 5° only, and were placed forward and aft of the funnels.

While *Normandie* had been in the early stages of being fitted out preparations were being made, in harbours on both sides of the Atlantic, to accommodate her. The harbour at Le Havre, her homeport, was dredged and a new dock was constructed. It was over 2,000ft long and would allow, for example, both *Normandie* and *Île de France* to be berthed at the same time. A new railway station, the Gare Maritime, a massive structure of reinforced concrete, was built nearby to accommodate the passengers that would arrive from Paris. Meanwhile, five huge new piers, of over 1,000ft in length, were being built in New York, that would accommodate not only *Normandie* but the other prestigious liners that were also being built by other nations as well.

By September 1934 the fitting out of *Normandie* was progressing at such a rate that CGT decided it was time to announce the date of her maiden voyage – 29 May 1935. However, it appeared that not everyone was filled with joy and pride as the magnificent liner began to come to life. In January, with just four months to go until her completion, a shipyard supervisor discovered loose wall panels in the ship. Looking further, he found evidence of what could only have been an attempt to sabotage the ship. There were needles sticking out of conduits and in other places conduits had been cut or completely removed. Had there been a fire as a result of these short-circuits *Normandie* could have been totally destroyed. Repairs were made and security around *Normandie* was intensified but the saboteur was never discovered. Not long

The Tourist Class Lounge.

afterward, Normandie was towed from her fitting out berth to the Joubert dry dock to have her propellers fitted.

Fully completed, the overall length of Normandie, from the bow to extreme aft, was 1,029ft 4in, with a beam of 117ft 9in at Main Deck. When fully loaded with passengers, stores, fresh water, crew and the like, she displaced 66,400tons, and in this condition drew 36ft 7in draft. Her gross tonnage was, at the time of her entry into service, 79,283, and the capacity of her fuel bunkers was 339,000cu.ft.

By this time there were over 6,000 workers involved in making Normandie ready for her sea trials, and as the date approached there still remained uncompleted public rooms and cabins. Nevertheless, it had been announced that the magnificent liner, that had grown to dominate the Penhoet skyline for three years, would depart on 5 May on her sea trials. Thousands of people packed the waterfront at St Nazaire all day to see her. Smoke had been wafting from her huge red, black-topped, funnels, and tugs bustled around her in an almost tantalising manner. Then, at last, at 5 p.m. Normandie began to move, guided by the tugs, she slowly and majestically steamed out of the fitting-out basin towards the open sea, escorted by two destroyers.

Quite apart from her officers, and managers of both CGT and the shipyard, Normandie had aboard an army of painters, decorators, upholsterers, carpenters and electricians, all of whom worked day and night throughout the trials to complete her fitting out. Although a full six days of trials were planned everyone aboard was anxious for Normandie to undertake one speed trial on that first evening. Remarkably, even with some of her boilers still cold, on that squally night she reached 24 knots with consummate ease. Various other trials of machinery and equipment, as well as countless exercises took place over the following days. On the second of her speed trials she reached 28 knots and later, to the delight of all those assembled on her bridge, she achieved 30.156 knots. It was then that her master, Capt. Pugnet, announced that Normandie had reached this remarkable speed still with some of her boilers cold! Further speed trials were run and she ultimately attained 32.125 knots, at 170,000hp. Normandie had in fact surpassed expectations – not only with her speed but, with her exceptional manoeuvrability and the fact that she consumed less fuel than Île de France. (It is also interesting to note that the Italian liner, Rex, had burned 1,100 tons of fuel a day when steaming at just under 30 knots whereas Normandie burned 950 tons at the same speed). Unfortunately, these speeds came at a high price – severe vibration was experienced in the after part of the ship, particularly on the upper decks (the location of her most prestigious accommodation).

At the completion of the trials Normandie arrived, as scheduled, in Le Havre at 7 p.m. on 11 May, in triumph. Crowds of people lined the dock and waterfront to greet her, boats and ships in the harbour blasted their sirens in welcome. Meanwhile, behind the scenes the shipyard workers laboured feverishly to install stanchions and deck stiffening in an attempt to limit the vibration. More visibly, the craftsmen that had accompanied her on the trials voyage were still aboard, working to get the great ship ready for her highly publicised maiden voyage. The CGT officials were confident that everything would be completed in time and that Normandie would sail on schedule. Then, on 20 May her crew joined a seamen's strike over wages. The official line to the crew was that any attempt to interfere with Normandie's maiden voyage would be regarded as a disloyal act. Fortunately, the dispute was quickly settled. In the early hours of the following day a watchman encountered two painters running away from an officer's cabin where they had been working. When he looked into the cabin there was a can of gasoline ablaze, just inches from the drapes. He was able to extinguish the fire and no damage had been done. The painters, when found, said they had been running to sound the alarm and French Line played the incident down as an accident caused by an inadvertently disposed of cigarette. Nevertheless, attempted sabotage was rumoured.

On 23 May the President of France, Albert Lebrun, hosted the very first gala event to be held aboard Normandie. Two thousand guests, the very cream of society along with representatives from the arts, politics and the sciences, were brought from Paris. They inspected the vast new Gare Maritime as they disembarked from their trains and made their way aboard the glittering new liner. Amongst them was Sir Percy Bates, the chairman of Cunard White Star Line. Even though his company's impressive new liner, which had been launched the previous September as the *Queen Mary*, was nearing completion he can have only been impressed by her French rivals' richness and modernity. There was, unfortunately, one very notable omission from the guest list, Vladimir Yourkevitch. Sadly, while the Penhoet shipyard and the owners of *Normandie*, CGT, had accepted his hull design they had been rather reluctant to accept the man himself. *Normandie* was intended to be a showcase of all that was grand and glorious about France – admitting that the most significant contribution to the construction and performance of the ship, the design of her hull, was by a Russian immigrant was not seen as glorification for France. Thus, his name never appeared in any press release about the ship. However, the fact did get leaked to the press – by his wife, and as a result the somewhat embarrassed French Line gave them a free round-trip on the maiden voyage, as a 'token of their gratitude'.

Further festivities followed in those final days before *Normandie* actually set sail for New York but the most glittering event of them all was held on 25th – a fund-raising benefit in aid of the Seamen's Fund and for the unemployed. The event, which ultimately became a tradition, included the special round-trip train from Paris to Le Havre, dinner, an entertainment in the theatre and the Grand Lounge, followed by a ball, was attended by all the very best known names in the aristocracy. Even on the very morning of her long awaited maiden voyage *Normandie* had one final wave of guests, travel agents from all over France and from neighbouring countries. As much as any the ultimate success of *Normandie* rested with them. However, in the middle of their visit, and shortly before they were about to be served a sumptuous lunch, *Normandie* lost all electrical power. Everything stopped – the winches loading luggage, the lifts and most importantly, at that moment, the kitchen ovens! It took an hour before power was restored. Initial thoughts had been sabotage but it turned out to have been caused by an over sensitive device designed to activate as soon as it detected a power anomaly.

Even in those final hours before *Normandie* embarked her first fare-paying passengers workmen were still frantically trying to get the ship finished. Many of them would have to remain aboard for that first voyage, making the finishing touches to mostly the cabins in Tourist and Third Class. Those classes were not fully booked but as First Class was almost full, for both voyages, westward and eastward, all attention had been focused on getting them as near perfect as possible. Even at that eleventh hour work continued to remedy the vibration problems.

The Tourist Class Dinning Room.

NORMANDIE

As the hour of her departure neared the worry about vibration problems and suspected sabotage attempts faded. *Normandie* sparkled with the freshness of her red, white and black paintwork in the bright afternoon sun, several tugs nudged into position in readiness to guide her out of the harbour and at 4 p.m. the call came for all visitors to go ashore but an hour later, when she had been due to sail, *Normandie* was still alongside. The delay had been caused by an incredible quantity of US bound mail that had descended on Le Havre, and all of it had to be franked before it could be brought aboard the ship. There were 1,276 passengers aboard for this first voyage: 830 in First Class, 308 in Tourist and just 123 in Third, served by a crew of 1,335. Over 50,000 spectators had crowded into Le Havre to watch her departure and at last, at 6.19 p.m., the ropes having been let go fore and aft, and with a great blast from her siren, *Normandie* was eased away from her berth. Her French Line fleet mates, *Île de France* and *Paris,* and the United States Lines *Manhattan* roared salutes in response, the crowds cheered, and then safely underway the tugs dropped astern. *Normandie* was on her own, her maiden voyage had begun.

Shortly after eleven that night she anchored off Southampton, she was a blaze of lights, her funnels floodlit and her name in huge

Top: On 5 May 1935, Normandie *departed St Nazaire for sea trials.*

Above and opposite: 11 May 1935, Le Havre – Normandie *arrives in triumph.*

Right: Sweeping curves of Normandie's *superstructure.*

illuminated letters between the second and third funnels. Tenders brought out embarking passengers, the Mayor of Southampton and members of the press. Some passengers, guests of French Line, disembarked here and by 3 a.m. *Normandie* was again underway. At ten the next morning she passed the famous Bishop's Rock lighthouse, the eastern point from which the speed across the Atlantic was calculated. However, French Line were denying that *Normandie* was out to break any records on this first voyage. Nevertheless, as each day passed so her speed increased and the ship was charged with an additional excitement. Her best day's run from noon to noon was as much as 754 miles, the average speed over this twenty-four hour period being 29.92 knots, and the highest speed recorded on this run was 31.37 knots. It was not, however, turning out to be a totally flawless voyage – while the strengthening to remedy the vibration problem had worked to some extent, it was nevertheless still evident. Also, some trouble was experienced with the main condenser tubes in one of the four main condensers of the big turbo-alternators. This made it necessary to cut out that particular alternator while repairs to the tubes were made. Fortunately, being a turbo-electric ship all four screws could still be kept running during this time, which would not have been the case with a more conventional geared turbine vessel.

By 2 June everyone was sure that *Normandie* had captured the Blue Riband, then on the final day of the voyage *Normandie* encountered fog. Capt. Pugnet radioed all ships in the vicinity and then maintained full speed, sure that there was no vessel near to cause any concern. Although she was not due alongside her New York pier until mid-after-

A pride of liners: Paris, Normandie *and* Île de France *at Le Havre.*

noon Pugnet maintained the speed throughout the night and in the early morning light, with New York just beyond the horizon, she was greeted by several small aircraft. At 11.02 a.m. *Normandie* passed the Ambrose Lightship, and as she did so she gave a tremendous blast on her siren. She had crossed the Atlantic from the Bishop's Rock lighthouse, in just four days, three hours and two minutes, at an average speed of 29.98 knots. *Normandie* had grasped the legendary Blue Riband from the Italian liner, *Rex*. Although French Line had made those denials at any record breaking attempt, almost as soon as the ship had passed the Ambrose Light stewards circulated amongst the passengers, giving out small *Normandie* pins, each decorated with a little blue ribbon and from the top of her after mast a giant blue pennant, 30m long – a metre for each knot of speed – was unfurled. There had been little doubt back in Le Havre about *Normandie*'s capability of capturing the record from the *Rex*.

A vast number of enthusiastic pressmen boarded *Normandie* as she lay off Quarantine and Madame Lebrun gave a brief speech about how pleased she was to have christened the ship and to have been aboard for the maiden voyage. Already, as *Normandie* began her slow approach up towards her Hudson River berth, the waters of the harbour and the skies above Manhattan began to buzz with excitement: excursion steamers, rowing boats, yachts and other private craft began to accompany her and there were the harbour fireboats sending up their welcoming plumes of water. Above there were dozens of aircraft buzzing back and forth across the spectacle and it was all being filmed and photographed from a team aboard a Goodyear airship, and crowds of spectators thronged the waterfront. Eventually, at 3.55 p.m., *Normandie* was securely alongside her New York berth for the first time.

The New York newspapers covered her arrival, and every possible aspect of *Normandie* in depth, and for the following four days she was the big news story. Several glittering and glamorous parties, galas and charity events were held aboard, each one of them attended by the cream of New York society along with the stars of both Broadway and Hollywood. Famous American orchestras and dance bands played at these events, including the exotic Xavier Cugat, whose orchestra played rumbas and tangos, rhythms that seemed to typify the sensuous elegance of *Normandie* herself. The ship was also open on one occasion to the general public and such was the excitement generated by the ship that it appeared that almost all of the visitors managed to find for themselves a souvenir of one form or another.

Once the reports had been received in Europe that *Normandie* had captured the Blue Riband the Master of the Italia liner, *Rex*, Cdr Francesco Tarabotto, sent a cable to Capt. Pugnet:

Our sincere admiration for a splendid ship and a remarkable performance on her maiden voyage enables us to relinquish with a smile our possession of the Blue Riband of the North Atlantic won two years ago.

Sadly, Germany was not as gracious as Italy, perhaps because they had initially been under the impression that *Normandie* had not made a record crossing. Nevertheless, fate would in the end have a curious way of repaying their ungracious behaviour.

Normandie departed New York on 7 June, with an almost capacity passenger load, and this also turned out to be a record-breaking crossing. Her average speed for the voyage was 30.31 knots, and it was the

Left: The President of France, Albert Lebrun, at the first gala to be held aboard.

Above and right: Glittering society aboard the glittering new liner.

NORMANDIE

first time that any liner had crossed the Atlantic at a better than 30 knots average. Without doubt, the maiden voyage had been a spectacular success! On her third crossing to New York *Normandie* had amongst her passengers the famous diplomat and writer, Harold Nicholson and his son, Ben. Harold Nicholson's observations of the voyage have often been quoted but he captured well the distinctly unreal quality of life in such luxurious surroundings:

Choruses of stewards, sailors, firemen, stewardesses, engineers and passengers. There are also some 50 liftiers in bright scarlet who look like the petals of salvias flying about these golden corridors. That is

the essential effect – gold, Lalique glass and scarlet. It is very gay, but would drive me mad after a week.

It was thus hardly surprising that he found the more severe, Bauhaus-inspired Café-Grill 'the nicest part of the ship'. Nicholson also noted that both he and Ben were finding it difficult to work or read a serious book and he said: 'There is something about a boat which upsets one's brain.'

Despite being the newest, most glamorous, most luxurious and certainly the fastest liner on the North Atlantic *Normandie* was not attracting the upper classes of the British travelling public. They were,

Above: Normandie *departs Le Havre on her maiden voyage.*

Left: Capt. Rene Pugnet and Staff Capt. Pierre Thoreaux.

Below: Capt. Pugnet and his officers on the bridge.

NORMANDIE

Top left: *Proudly flying her flags.*

Above: *Passengers line the Boat Deck...*

Left: *...and the Promenade Deck.*

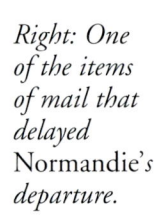

Right: *One of the items of mail that delayed Normandie's departure.*

officers on her bridge, the bridge wings were enlarged and also extended forward by three feet. The large illuminated letters that spelled out her name between the funnels were removed. In the Grand Dining Room six of the twelve elaborate lighting towers were removed to create more space in the room. The two-deck high Tourist Class lounge was removed and in its place thirty-two new cabins were created. To replace this lounge CGT created what was probably the most spectacular Tourist Class lounge ever, but in doing so somewhat compromised the purity of *Normandie*'s profile. A whole new structure to house the lounge was built aft on Boat Deck, thereby eliminating the elegant terrace deck, with its zigzag benches. A sports deck, for Tourist Class was created on the deck above the new lounge. The magnificent view aft over *Normandie*'s wake, which First Class passengers had formerly enjoyed from the exclusive Café-Grill, was now the privilege of the Tourist Class passengers to enjoy instead. Also, from their newly created Sports Deck those in Tourist Class had an unobstructed view of the private verandahs of the Deauville and Trouville Suites – much

Left: Albert Brenet's impression of a North Atlantic crossing.

Below: On that first voyage it was warm enough for passengers to enjoy Normandie's *open decks.*

in the main, staying loyal to British ships, and this caused the CGT officials some degree of concern. In her first few voyages most of her First Class passengers had been American – from both the rather grand New York society and from the more racy and glamorous Hollywood crowd. In an attempt to promote *Normandie* to the British market CGT created a gap in her Atlantic schedule to enable her to undertake what would be her first cruise – around the British Isles. It was a cruise of just three nights – from 19 to 22 July – and fares were set at 800F in First Class, 700F in Tourist Class and 550F in what the publicity material described as being 'classe speciale'. Over 1,700 French tourists took advantage of this unique opportunity. *Normandie* arrived in Southampton on 21 July and thousands of visitors swarmed aboard her. Three days later she resumed her transatlantic schedule. Unfortunately, the problems with vibration continued to plague her and CGT decided to cut short her first Atlantic season, cancelling the voyages after her arrival in Le Havre on 28 October, so that they could attempt to find a solution.

What resulted was an expensive, lengthy and quite a radical refit, indeed, in part it was even a rebuild. After a series of trials voyages it was ascertained that first and foremost, her propellers should be replaced with new ones of a four-bladed design. In a move to aid the

NORMANDIE

Left: The tourist deck swimming pool.

Rightt: Glamorous passengers dancing in the Café-Grill.

Below: Drinks by the indoor pool bar.

to the dismay of movie queen, Marlene Dietrich, on one occasion. The creation of the lounge, and the harm it brought to the ship's overall appearance, was an unhappy necessity brought about by the need to stiffen the ship in order to help rid her of the vibration problem. Elsewhere, 80 tons of steel were added to her stern, to stiffen the decks and reinforce shaft bossings. To counter this, 200tons of pig iron was added to her forward ballast tanks to keep her in trim. In total the work had cost CGT 150,000,000F, but as far as they were concerned it was money well spent in order to maintain the prestige of their flagship, and therefore the prestige of France.

As a result of the work and the creation of the new lounge *Normandie* was remeasured and was now 83,423gt, a fact that came as something of a blow to Cunard-White Star. They had proudly announced that upon entering service the *Queen Mary* would be 80,773gt. *Normandie* remained for a while longer, therefore, the largest, longest and the fastest liner in the world, and as she proved in another trials voyage in April on completion of the work, she was now vibration free as well. CGT were ecstatic and the French Line advertising department commissioned lavish press advertisements promoting 'The vibrationless *Normandie*' and 'The Perfect Ship' and the like. However, unknowingly, disaster had struck. It was discovered, less than 24 hours before she was due to sail on her first voyage of the 1936 season, that one of the new propellers had inexplicably fallen off! The company had no option but to reinstall the 'old' ones until a new replacement could be made,

Normandie's triumphant arrival in New York.

as the ship could not function with an unbalanced set of propellers. Thus, to everyone's disappointment as *Normandie* set sail for New York it was apparent that to some extent the vibration was still evident. The additional steel work and new structure alone was not enough to rid her of the problem. By the time that *Normandie* was back in Le Havre the replacement propeller had been recast and at last the vibrationless *Normandie* was a reality.

The solution to the problem was timely, as barely ten days later the long-awaited Cunard-White Star liner, *Queen Mary*, entered service. However, she broke no records on her maiden voyage but like *Normandie* she also suffered from vibration problems. Although viewed as competitors, the ships created their own loyal followers and appealed to different types of people. Those who sailed aboard *Normandie* tended to view the new Cunarder as dowdy by comparison. Though there was no denying her stately appearance she was little more than a refined version of the *Aquitania*, giving her a profile little different to the liners she was designed to replace. Whereas *Normandie* was decorated with rich fabrics and luxurious materials the *Queen Mary* presented a more quiet style, relying on exotic woods from every part of the British Empire for her decorative effects, also much use was made of plastic in her fittings (then a revolutionary new material). Plastic, however, was not used at all aboard *Normandie*. Nevertheless, to create the opulence of *Normandie* had cost the equivalent of almost $60 million, nearly twice that of the *Queen Mary*. So it was inevitable that the new Cunarder would suffer in comparison.

NORMANDIE

Above and left: A flotilla of all manner of craft were there to greet her.

Below: Thousands of people lined the waterfront.

Vladimir Yourkevitch had two photographs in his office that he would always proudly show to visitors. Both were aerial views, one of *Normandie* and the other one of the *Queen Mary,* both at speed. He would point out the lack of turbulence along *Normandie*'s hull in contrast to the lather of white water created all around the *Queen Mary*. He would also explain that in order for the *Queen Mary* to obtain that additional fraction of a knot of speed to enable her to outrun *Normandie* she needed an additional forty thousand horsepower.

In June 1936 *Normandie* was involved in a rather curious accident while at anchor off Southampton. A small seaplane, from the RAF station at Gosport, had been buzzing low over the liner when one of its wings clipped one of her working deck cranes. The pilot tried to maintain control of the plane but it crashed onto the foredeck. Very fortunately the pilot walked away uninjured.

It was just two months later; in August that *Normandie* briefly lost her title of Blue Riband holder of the Atlantic, to the *Queen Mary*. It was perhaps appropriate that the *Queen Mary* should have gained the record on this occasion as she had amongst her passengers the Olympic runner, Jesse Owens, who was returning in triumph to America from the Berlin Olympics with his gold medal. On 31 August *Queen Mary* also broke the record for the eastbound crossing. That winter *Normandie* was again refitted. French Line had every intention of winning back the honour of being the fastest ship on the Atlantic. Extra steam nozzles were installed in her boiler room to boost power output, the size of the pipes that supplied steam to her turbines were increased and once again her propellers were replaced. They were similar in design to the others but were smaller and were built to revolve faster, allowing the engines to develop more horsepower.

On 19 March the Manhattan piers held a fabulous array of record-breaking ocean liners: along with *Normandie* were the *Europa* and the *Rex*, both former Blue Riband holders and Cunard's *Berengaria*, once the largest liner in the world. Departing from this illustrious company *Normandie*'s new master, Capt. Thoreaux

Mme Lebrun receives the keys of the city of New York.

(Capt. Pugnet having retired the previous summer) decided to put her new mechanical refinements to the test. *Normandie* excelled herself, not only did she capture the Blue Riband but she maintained, on several occasions, the remarkable speed of 33 knots. Five months later, on 2 August, she arrived in New York proudly flying the Blue Riband pennant once more; having made the crossing in just three days twenty-three hours and two minutes, and this was despite having to steam through a severe storm with head winds of over 70 mph. Her return to Europe was another record-breaking run, even faster than her crossing back in March.

Back in April CGT had announced that during February 1938 *Normandie* would undertake another cruise, only this time it would be a rather more extravagant affair than her first one – the long weekend around the British Isles. This would be a twenty-one-day excursion to the Caribbean and South America. The cruise was arranged in conjunction with the renowned Raymond-Whitcomb Travel Agency and it was agreed that *Normandie* would operate as a 'one class' ship and that her passenger capacity would be limited to 1,000. The cruise was sold out within just two weeks of it being announced. Fares ranged from $9,970 for either the Deauville or the Trouville Suites (if occupied by eight people) down to a twin cabin in what was normally designated Tourist Class, for $790. While there were other luxurious liners employed at the time on lengthy winter cruises there was nothing to compare with the cruise aboard *Normandie*. It was the cruise event of the season; newspapers carried pictures of the departure, and a broadcast from the Grand Salon was carried across America. She departed New York on 5 February and made stops at Nassau and Trinidad before arriving in Rio de Janeiro for a five-day stay. On her return to New

Above: The new Queen of the North Atlantic.

Right: Tennis being played during a 1936 voyage.

York *Normandie* called at Martinique. For the added entertainment of her privileged passengers *Normandie* carried a lecturer, two bridge instructors, two dance instructors (from one of the best New York studios, naturally), several professional dancers of the stage and nightclubs, and singers who were popular in concert programmes and on the radio.

The cruise was described as being like 'living in a fairy-tale' and apparently the spectacle of this remarkable liner at anchor in the Caribbean brought crowds of natives from all over the islands just to see her. The 'fairy-tale', however, had its shortcomings: *Normandie* had never been designed with tropic cruising in mind; she was an Atlantic liner pure and simple. Thus, as she neared the Equator the broad sweep of forward facing windows turned the Winter Garden into a greenhouse, and the plants and flowers that had flourished in the more temperate northerly latitudes suffered in the heat. The small outdoor swimming pool, down on the Tourist Class after deck was constantly crowded but its lack of surrounding lido area hardly made it a place to lounge around. Even so, on 12 February it was certainly the focus of much attention when the traditional 'crossing of the line' ceremony was held. This was a particularly significant occasion of course as it was also the first time that *Normandie* herself had 'crossed the line'.

In July *Normandie* made her one-hundredth crossing of the Atlantic. Her average speed during these crossings was 28.54 knots. The French Line publicity department also announced at the time that she had used 590,798 tons of oil and her passengers had consumed 572,519 bottles of wine and champagne. The following month she ultimately relinquished her title of Blue Riband holder to the *Queen Mary*. Though in the congratulatory message sent by *Normandie*'s relief Master to the Master of the *Queen Mary*, was the statement: 'Bravo! To the *Queen Mary* until the next time.' The rivalry between the two ships had captured the public's imagination but although she had lost the 'speed Queen' title *Normandie* retained the allure of the glamour ship, the ship whose passenger lists were studded with the more glittering international celebrities.

Above left: With her Blue Riband pennant flying, Normandie *returns to Le Havre.*

Above: Normandie's *first cruise.*

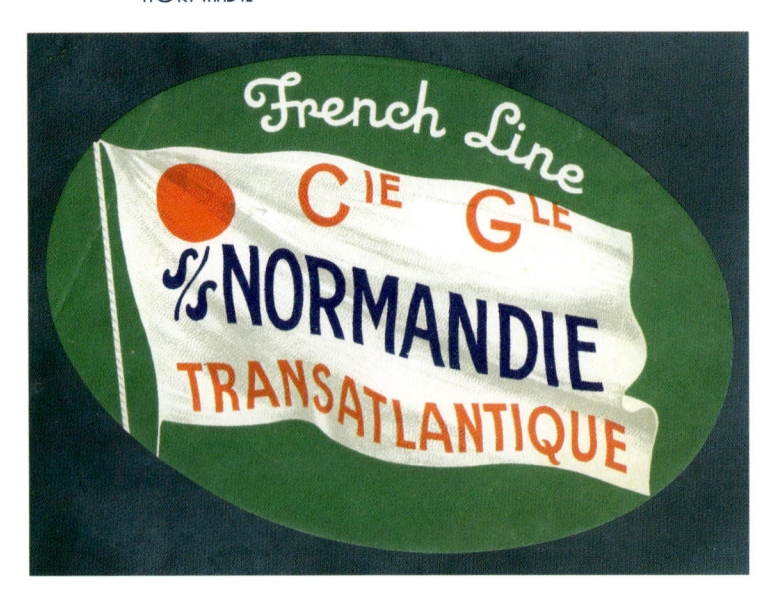

Above: The sundeck of the Normandie.

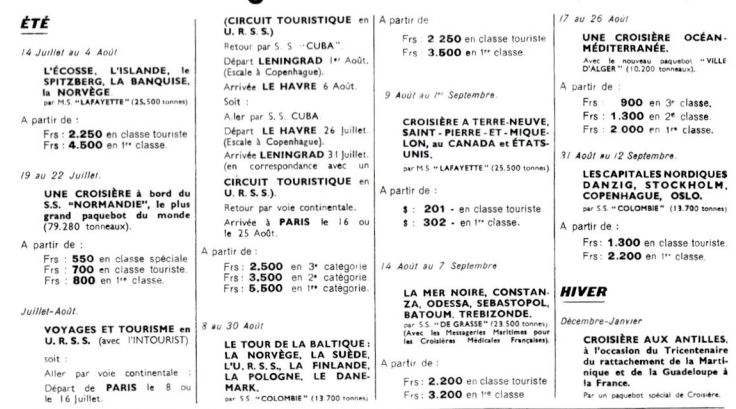

In those one-hundred or so crossings *Normandie*'s name came to suggest the best in ocean transportation, so that when a film wished to portray an Atlantic voyage in the grand manner there were likely to be flashes of the great ship arriving or departing New York. However, as though echoing those earlier statements by Harold Nicholson, for some her grandeur was just too overwhelming, her luxury just too hedonistic, her décor just too rich.

Right and below right: The newest, most glamorous, most luxurious and the fastest liner on the North Atlantic.

Below: Normandie *prepares for another voyage.*

Bottom: Normandie *probably on her first cruise around Britain.*

NORMANDIE

It seemed that the very concept of the grand luxe aura was enough to make potential passengers turn instead to her running mate, *Île de France*, which had her own very distinct personality and intensely loyal following. As a consequence, although *Normandie* did manage some impressive passenger loads (1,831 being the largest number of passengers she ever carried, during a crossing in 1937) she often sailed well below capacity. For example in 1935 she averaged 993 passengers per crossing, not a particularly impressive figure for a new Blue Riband-winning liner. The following year her average passenger loads per crossing dropped even

Top: Normandie, en mer.

Above: The broad Boat Deck, with room for two rows of deck chairs.

Above right: Clay pigeon shooting from the deck.

Right: Normandie *leaving Manhattan.*

Opposite: The ultimate ship in a bottle! Normandie's *image was widely used in advertising, from fuel oil to an aperitif.*

64

LINER OF LEGEND

NORMANDIE

Passengers aboard Île de France *gaze in awe at the magnificent* Normandie.

Opposite top left: The new Tourist Class lounge dominated her aft superstructure.

Opposite left: Normandie, *believed to be at anchor off Southampton. Note the baggage being trans-shipped using a forward derrick.*

LINER OF LEGEND

Cie Générale Transatlantique. Paquebot «NORMANDIE». Départ du HAVRE. Les Plages Arrière. (longueur 313 m. largeur 36 m. 40. force 160 000 chx. vitesse 30 nœuds.)

French Line C.G.T.
SOUTHAMPTON TO NEW YORK
EXPRESS LUXURY SERVICE
"ILE DE FRANCE" "NORMANDIE"
ENQUIRE WITHIN

67

lower, to 908 but in 1937 they were a little better, at 1,043. Whilst *Normandie* was the liner that had all the glamour and Parisian *chic*, it was the *Queen Mary* that had the high passenger loads. In 1936 *Normandie* carried a total of 27,292 passengers on thirty Atlantic crossings against the *Queen Mary*, which carried 42,032.

The success of the Rio cruise was such that CGT and Raymond-Whitcomb were inspired to repeat it in 1939, and in September 1938 they issued a lavish, thirty-two-page brochure to promote it. This time the cruise would be slightly longer, twenty-four days, and while the itinerary would be the same it would also include a call at Barbados. The stay in Rio would coincide with the first two days of the famous Carnival. The cruise had all the excitement and glamour of the previous one and it was as a direct result of this cruise that Hollywood would acquire one of its most remarkable and highly individual musical stars. The theatrical impresario, Lee Shubert, was one of the passengers aboard *Normandie*, and while in Rio he went to the city's premier nightclub, Casino Orca. It was there that he heard a singer, Maria do Carmo Miranda da Conha perform. He was so impressed by her beauty and her unique talent that he signed her and took her to New York. Her name was shortened to Carmen Miranda, and a star was born. The cruise was, perhaps, *Normandie*'s last glittering moment in the spotlight – a final dazzling appearance before the world descended into chaos.

Back in Le Havre, in April, *Normandie* was undergoing dry-docking when on the 19th a fire broke out aboard her fleet mate, *Paris*, which was being readied for a voyage to New York. In fighting the fire the fireboats inundated the liner with water to such an extent that she capsized. It was necessary for her masts to be removed to enable *Normandie* to move out of the dry dock.

Above: Passengers gather on deck to watch the 'crossing of the line' ceremony.

Left: 'Cruise ship' Normandie.

NORMANDIE

GROSS TONNAGE
79,280

The NORMANDIE
THE WORLD'S LARGEST SHIP

LENGTH
1029 FEET

LINER OF LEGEND

Normandie *at anchor off Rio during the 1938 cruise.*

NORMANDIE

At the time all of Europe was buzzing with the talk of the probability of war; indeed, even the fire aboard the *Paris* had turned out to be an act of sabotage, and many of *Normandie*'s westbound passengers were refugees and others fleeing the disturbing influences of Nazism. Against this worrying backdrop CGT made the announcement that they intended to build a sister ship to *Normandie*, she would however, be larger and slightly more powerful, and that construction would begin in 1940. While announced as being a replacement for the lost *Paris* she was more likely to have been the result of the company rising to the challenge from Cunard, which already had under construction a liner that was a larger version of the *Queen Mary*.

On 23 August *Normandie* left Le Havre on her 139th transatlantic voyage. She would never see her homeport again. She arrived in New York on 28 August and had been scheduled to return to France the following day. The tension was such in Europe that a mere 350 passengers had booked to make the crossing. Her departure was delayed at first by just one day and then, indefinitely. No one realised at the time but the career of the world's most fabulous liner was at an end. Indeed, the curtain was about to come down on an era of unparalleled oceanic splendour.

Above: Another advertiser making use of the popular and glamourous image of the Normandie.

Right: A detail of the smoking room door.

72

FIVE
TRAGEDY

From August 1938 the Blue Riband would no longer fly from her mast.

LINER OF LEGEND

CGT, realising that the escalating conflict in Europe could result in *Normandie* having to stay in New York for years rather than months or weeks, ordered her to be mothballed. Her luxurious furnishings and fittings were draped in protective covers and the majority of her crew were returned to France. Among the duties of those remaining was to tend the plants and the birds in the Winter Garden but eventually, as *Normandie*'s stay in New York lengthened the birds were sold to a pet shop. Whilst her public areas resembled a ghost-ship down in the engine rooms all continued to be ready, in the unlikely case that the situation in Europe might change. Each engine was turned over for a month, in turn. By early 1940 her crew were further reduced to just 115, and in time more of these would also leave.

In the evening of 7 March the Cunard liner that might have been nearer to *Normandie*'s equal, *Queen Elizabeth*, made her dramatic entry into New York. Her near sister, *Queen Mary* was already there, thus the world's three largest liners were berthed together for the first, and only, time. The three beautiful Queens of the sea, but sadly, already in exile, for *Normandie* her reign was over.

The Cunarders left for their trooping duties and *Normandie* remained, looking more and more sad as the elements faded her once pristine livery. As the American government were concerned that somehow Nazi sympathisers might sabotage *Normandie*, it was decided that she should be given the protection of the United States Coast Guard, and in May 1941 Coast Guard personnel moved into the vacated crew

Fire rages aboard the liner Paris, *and arson is suspected.*

Normandie *trapped in drydock and an oil slick surrounds the devastated* Paris.

Opposite: A final look towards France....

quarters. On 12 December, the day after the United States had declared war on Germany, and five days after the Japanese attack on Pearl Harbour, America took possession of *Normandie*. Having taken control of the liner there was then some confusion and protracted discussion over what should be done with her, what would her most useful role be? Some were convinced that her immense length meant that she was most suited to conversion to an aircraft carrier but the fact that her hull was not armoured like that of a naval ship made the argument for her conversion into a troop transport, similar to the Cunard 'Queens', a much more sensible proposition.

Several warehouses were rented to accommodate *Normandie's* furnishings and fittings, and gradually she was stripped of all her finery. Everything was carefully removed with a view to it being reinstalled after the war. The work, however, was carried out swiftly as the plan was to have her carrying over 14,000 troops by the end of January. While the stripping of her interiors was being carried out her now faded French Line livery was painted over in a camouflage design in shades of grey, and the letters that spelled name on her bow and stern were removed. She was to be renamed *Lafayette* – the name that French Line had given one of her smaller 'cabin class' fleet mates in 1929, and which was destroyed by fire nine years later. The new name, however, was never painted on her bows and she continued to be known by everyone as *Normandie*. *Normandie's* once fabulous public rooms were slowly being transformed into mess halls, canteens or sleeping areas of stacked standee-bunks. While her interior was being transformed beyond recognition so was her exterior, with parts of her curving superstructure being disfigured by steel sheets and gallons of black paint.

The frantic need to meet the planned deadline resulted in some unfortunate results that would ultimately have dire consequences. On her bridge, fire alarm switches were disconnected while other work was undertaken there and were inadvertently not reconnected. Due to some Fire Department bureaucracy the ship-to-shore fire alarm box link ceased once the US Navy took control of the ship from French Line. None of the workers who stood watch during welding and burning operations had been given any training in fire fighting. To add to all the confusion, *Normandie* had initially been placed under the control of the US Navy, but as they had a shortage of manpower it was decided that she should be given to the Army. Nevertheless, it was decided that the Navy should complete the fitting out of the ship. There was then disagreement between the Army and its requirements and the Navy and what it thought was appropriate. In the end it was decided that the only solution was to return full control of the ship back to the Navy.

LINER OF LEGEND

NORMANDIE

Due to the enormity of the task and the confusion over responsibility, the January deadline passed with ship still in a turmoil of partly completed reconstruction. One of the multitude of tasks that had not been completed was the removal of the four steel columns, in what had been the Grand Lounge, which had supported the Lalique fountains of light. Work on their removal began on 9 February 1942, and by the early afternoon three had been removed and work began on the final one. Unfortunately, and perhaps due to the confusion and the frantic pace at which the gutting of *Normandie* had taken place, the Grand Lounge had been used as a storage area for hundreds of kapok-filled life jackets – all wrapped in equally flammable burlap. Also, perhaps due to a momentary lapse of concentration after a day spent cutting the stanchions, the workman was, for a few seconds, unaware that a flame had leapt from his cutting torch to the stacked bales of life jackets. The effect was instantaneous – 'Like a fire in dry grass' one of the men was later quoted. All efforts to put the fire out were fruitless and rapidly it was spreading and out of control. The call was put out to evacuate the ship but with over 3,000 men aboard her at the time this alone was not an easy task to effect. As the smoke began to penetrate the liner so many of the men were overcome by it and had to be rescued by either their workmates or the fire fighters.

Not only had fire engines arrived at the dockside but also fireboats arrived, but despite the vast quantities of water that they poured into the ship the entire superstructure soon appeared to be consumed by the fire. Within less than an hour of that first flame leaping from the cutting torch to the stacked life jackets most of the great public rooms for which *Normandie* had been famous were destroyed – albeit that they had already been stripped of their fine appointments. A huge pall of smoke drifted across Manhattan and word that *Normandie* was burning spread as quickly as the fire itself, and gradually the area around Pier 88 began to fill with thousands of sightseers, many of whom had seen her arrival in triumph. Now they stood in horror as this symbol of France, this most beautiful of ships, was slowly being consumed by fire. Its heat blistering the freshly applied camouflage paint so that it began peeling away, and in her death throes *Normandie* was attempting to shrug off the identity that her new masters had sought to impose upon her, and once more the bold red and black of her funnels proudly shone through, only to be engulfed in the acrid smoke.

Amongst the crowds was the designer of *Normandie*'s revolutionary hull, Vladimir Yourkevitch. He frantically tried

LINER OF LEGEND

Above: Three Queens of the Atlantic berthed together for the first, and only, time.

Opposite: Smoke from the fire appeared to engulf Manhattan.

to explain to a naval officer on duty who he was and of his special knowledge of the ship. He knew that he could help and he could see the inevitable happening if the fire engines and fire boats continued to pump so much water into her. Already she had taken on a severe list, her mooring ropes as tight as sprung steel and with each degree the stricken liner shuddered to port the crowd shouted in horrified fascination: 'She's going, she's going!'

Under the immense strain the ropes ripped mooring bollards from the dockside and gangways clattered free. Yourkevitch tried to explain that if the Navy were to let him aboard the ship he could open her sea-cocks allowing her to settle on the harbour bottom, secure and in an upright position. The officer turned to Yourkevitch and replied: 'The Navy's in charge, don't you worry about it, we know what to do.' Only Yourkevitch knew that they did not know and he could see that his beloved *Normandie* was dying – and *Normandie* did die.

NORMANDIE BURNS

NORMANDIE

Above and left: Inundated with water, fire ravaged Normandie *began to list.*

Through intrepid fire fighting *Normandie*'s engines, bridge and vital lower portions remained unscathed by the fire. It was hoped therefore that provided she could win the impending battle with the incoming tide, work would continue immediately on her conversion. At this time Navy officials termed the damage 'comparatively slight', but unofficial estimates placed its cost at $5,000,000. Weighted down with the water that the fire fighters had poured into her, *Normandie* was resting on the muddy bottom of her berth. It was expected that the incoming tide would refloat her but this raised the possibility that she would topple over unless sufficient water were drained from her upper decks to alleviate the list. The closing of all the fire doors to protect the lower decks had saved the vital areas of the ship from the blaze but it now proved to be a grave hazard. The doors prevented the tons of water in her upper superstructure from flowing down into the hull. Hence the dangerous list, due to top-heaviness. While crews of men attempted to pump out the water half a dozen tugs, churning the murky water with all their power, tried to push the stricken liner against the pier – preparing to try and hold it against the tide.

Shortly before 1 a.m. on 10 February the Admiral in charge ordered all hands to evacuate the ship, despite their work the list had increased to a critical 25°. The tugs were also ordered away, lest they be crushed as *Normandie* fell. Almost twelve hours after that first bale of life jackets had been ignited, at 2.37 a.m. on 10 February, deluged with water and listing at 33°, her final lines snapped and she slowly rolled onto her side into the dirty, ice-filled waters of the Hudson River.

In giving his reaction to the fire to the press, the French Ambassador said:

The burning of that ship will come as a terrible blow to the French people – she was the pride of France's maritime industry. It seems inconceivable that measures could not have been taken to prevent its destruction.

As with her maiden arrival in the port, the New York press were full of stories regarding *Normandie*'s destruction. One newspaper carried the words: '*Normandie* – monument to bungling inefficiency, stupidity.' Another newspaper carried a cartoon of the Statue of Liberty in tears.

Plans for *Normandie*'s salvage began immediately. However, to enable the ship to be brought upright anything that hindered her natural buoyancy had to be removed. Gradually, over the following weeks her spectacular funnels, those very symbols of *Normandie* herself, were cut away and then the work began on the removal of her superstructure. There was much discussion regarding what should be done with *Normandie* once she was refloated, it was even suggested that she might be scrapped where she lay. However, it was decided that her potential use in the war effort was worth the expense in refloating her and in fact Vladimir Yourkevitch was consulted on the best way that the refloating could be carried out. It was, however, a lengthy and difficult process, which was hindered by the fact that she had been severely dam-

Right: For a time hope remained that Normandie *would sail again.*

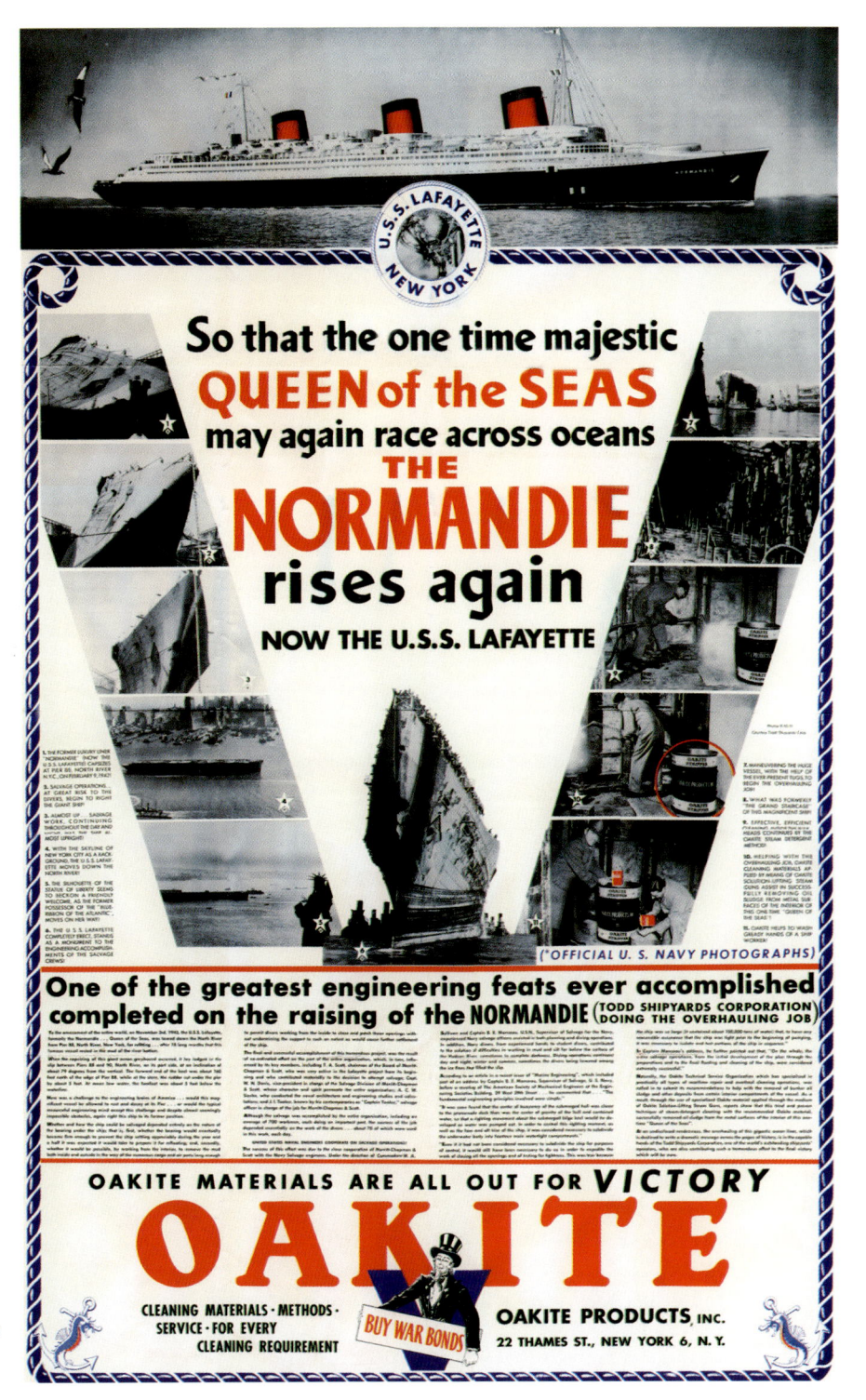

NORMANDIE

Clockwise from above: After eighteen months of dangerous work the wreck of Normandie *was finally refloated.*

aged by a knob of rock on the harbour bed upon which the submerged hull had pivoted during the ebb and flow of each tide. Two further fires broke out during the salvage work, one on 13 March 1942 and another one, much more serious, two months later on 18 May. It had been started by sparks from a blowtorch and took several hours to be put out. It was not until the early hours of 15 September 1943 that the remains that once were *Normandie,* were again afloat. Regardless of the fact that she was now but a battered hulk, plans progressed to repair her for service – the war effort demanded it. Now it was not a case of whether she would be either a troop transport or an aircraft carrier; she would be both – a troop transport that could not only carry men and vehicles but also aircraft, which could fly on and off her deck.

On 3 November *Normandie* was ready to leave her pier, for the first time in four years, albeit under the care of several tugs. *Normandie* was expected to remain in the dry dock for three weeks before the actual rebuilding would begin, but things did not turn out as planned. Once out of the water it was obvious that the damage to her hull was far more severe than anticipated and further inspection revealed, not unsurprisingly, that almost all of her propulsion machinery had been ruined beyond repair by their months of submersion. This was a fact that seemed not to have been considered during the long salvage process and the discussions for her

84

LINER OF LEGEND

Upright again, the beautiful hull once more towers above Pier 88.

future role. Therefore, for her to sail again she would need entirely new machinery and the enormity of this revelation changed all the plans entirely. Nevertheless, her hull was made sound and in January 1944 she was towed to a berth in Brooklyn and there she waited for the Navy and the government to decide her fate. There were countless plans, including the possibility of her being rebuilt as a passenger liner once the war was over. These plans all came to nothing and the hulk of what was once the glorious *Normandie* was all but forgotten, until June 1945, a month after VE Day, when the head of the US Maritime Commission offered to resell the

NORMANDIE

Above: Normandie *leaves her pier for the first time in four years.*

Opposite: *The wreck of the former pride of France is towed to Brooklyn to await her fate.*

hulk to France. It was not until October that the French Ambassador responded: 'CGT does not intent to repurchase *Normandie*, but are ready to contemplate with the American authorities a legitimate compensation in suitable tonnage.' The US government were far from pleased by this response. Despite further attempts to sell it no one else had any use for the hulk either, so it was put up for sale as scrap. It was bought for $3.80-a-ton by the Lipsett Corporation, and on 28 November 1946, with the name Lipsett emblazoned on the hull it was towed by twelve tugs to Port Newark.

By 7 October 1947 all that remained of *Normandie* was a 75-ton section of steel that had been part of her double bottom. A giant crane lifted this from the water and it was transported to a steel company in Pennsylvania, to be melted down.

Normandie was gone – a legend was born.

NORMANDIE

Longueur, 313 m. 75 ; Largeur, 35 m. 90 ; Vitesse, 30 nœuds. - Tirant d'eau moyen en charge : 11 m. 16 - Jauge brute ; 75.000 tonnes

U.S.S. LAFAYETTE
NEW YORK

88

SIX

IN NORMANDIE'S WAKE

Careworn but proud, Liberté *steams into Le Havre.*

In reality it was difficult to compensate CGT for the loss of *Normandie*, she had after all been quite unique. However, on 28 May 1946 an agreement was signed and America paid the French $13.5 million. It was also agreed, by the International Reparations Commission (due to American influence) and not without some considerable irony, that CGT should be awarded the former North German Lloyd liner, *Europa*, one of *Normandie*'s arch-rivals that had been seized by US troops.

Europa had spent the war years tied up at Bremerhaven and was to have been converted into a troop carrier for the planned invasion of Britain. Fortunately the conversion had never taken place so that when the American invasion forces arrived in Bremerhaven in May 1945 they found the very neglected and rusting liner, at the time the third largest liner in the world. She was given some temporary repairs and made some voyages returning troops back to the United States. However, as a result of her years of neglect and inactivity she was unreliable and susceptible to fires, so her troopship role came to a hasty end, and she was handed over to the International Reparations Commission.

In June 1946 she was handed over to CGT and although the name *Lorraine* had been considered she was given the singularly more appropriate te name, *Liberté*. Still looking careworn from her years of inactivity and only minor attention during her role as a troopship, CGT nevertheless had her funnels painted in red and black and she sailed for Le Havre. On 8 December, shortly after she had arrived, the port was struck by a fierce gale and *Liberté* was torn from her moorings and by some curious twist of fate was driven into the wreck of the *Paris* (that had remained in the harbour since April 1939) ripping her hull open. *Liberté* sank, but fortunately in an upright position. Whilst her salvage was given priority, *Liberté* was not refloated until 15 April 1947, and she was then towed to St Nazaire to be refitted.

Transforming the former pride of the German merchant marine into a suitable replacement for *Normandie* was a monumental task, quite apart from the damage that had been done to the liner during her months resting on the bottom of Le Havre harbour. The work took over two years to complete and was estimated to have cost in excess of $19 million. In October 1949, just as the work was nearing completion a fire broke out aboard the ship, which damaged her freshly restored interiors and thus even further delayed her entry into service. *Liberté*, looking every inch a French Line flagship, arrived for the first time in New York harbour on 17 August 1950, to the usual maiden voyage reception of hooting tugs and plumes of spray from accompanying fireboats. Eight days later, as *Liberté* made her way down the Hudson River, on the return leg of her maiden voyage she passed the inbound *Île de France*. French Line were back in business!

Île de France had also spent over two years being refitted after years of war work, and eventually returned to service in July 1949. Both *Liberté* and *Île de France* were, in part, decorated and furnished with items from *Normandie*. For example: the centre section of the huge carpet that had once graced *Normandie*'s Grand Lounge was placed

Liberté's *First Class Smoking Room decorated with panels from the Smoking Room aboard* Normandie.

Crowds line the waterfront as Liberté *departs on her maiden voyage.*

in the Cabin Class Drawing Room aboard *Île de France*, also, one of the panels, 'Fishing' from *Normandie*'s Smoke Room was placed in her Grand Salon and part of the remarkable glass panels from *Normandie*'s Grand Lounge, which were entitled 'Dawn, the Four Winds and the Sea', was installed in her Smoke Room. Perhaps, in an even more concerted effort to erase all of her German styling and totally imbue the ship with a French character, *Liberté* was even more lavishly graced with decorative panels and furnishings from *Normandie*. Her First Class Grand Salon, whilst not exactly a replica of the one aboard her predecessor, had some of the panels and

Île de France, still stately after a two-year refit.

furnishings from *Normandie*'s lounge and had that same golden and red glow, and the room even gave the impression of being of the same proportions. Panels from *Normandie*'s Smoke Room, 'Harvesting', were installed in *Liberte*'s Smoking Room and elsewhere through the ship other items were installed. Aboard both *Liberte* and *Île de France* the china, glass and silverware as well as linens from *Normandie* were also used.

It is very unfortunate that a very large proportion of *Normandie*'s furnishings and artworks were never returned to France. Instead much of her exquisite furniture was sold off in auctions in America during the 1940's, ultimately finding homes in the most remarkable of locations, from churches to hotels and restaurants to supermarkets. Baudry's statue, La Normandie, which had been in the Smoking Room, was bought for Our Lady of Lebanon church, in Brooklyn, along with the bronze doors that had lead into the Grand Dining Room, and the cloisonné panels of a Norman knight. The statue, however, was sold again and stood for many years in the Fountainbleu Hotel in Miami. However, in June 2001 it was announced that the statue had been sold to Celebrity Cruises, to be installed in the main dining room aboard their 90,000gt cruise ship, *Summit*, which was then under construction. Celebrity had also acquired some of the panels from *Normandie*'s Smoking Room to grace the walls of an exclusive restaurant elsewhere aboard *Summit*.

The other statue, La Paix, which had stood in *Normandie*'s Grand Dining Room, has ended up in what is called the Garden of Normandie in a memorial park on Long Island. The double doors, and the surrounding panels, that separated *Normandie*'s Grand Lounge and Smoking Room, were installed in a New York restaurant.

LINER OF LEGEND

Above and below: The Grand Salon and the Writing Room aboard Île de France *decorated with panels from* Normandie.

Below right: A section of the carpet from Normandie's *Grand Lounge was used in the Cabin Class Drawing Room.*

Some of the furnishings and art works from *Normandie* were disposed of to hotels or other locations by French Line when first *Île de France* and then later, *Liberté*, were sold for scrap. Many items, originally aboard *Normandie*, were gathered together and sold at a prestigious auction, held in Monte Carlo in 1981 – all doubtless finding safe homes with avid collectors of fine art and enthusiasts of this incomparable liner. Several smaller decorative panels are now again at sea, having been installed aboard very large and luxurious private yachts.

Normandie's 620lb brass steam whistle, which had been carried on her forward funnel, found use for some years as a works hooter at a Pennsylvania steel plant. Later, it was used as a community fire alarm. Then, in June 1985 it was installed at the Ocean Liner Museum in New York.

It was not until February 1962 that *Normandie*'s true successor entered service and was named, *France*. Perhaps not as revolutionary in her design as *Normandie* but equally as beautiful, given that twenty-seven years separated them. Internally, *France* was equally as striking as *Normandie*, though there were few that felt that her stark and dramatic décor was the equal to the opulent décor of her predecessor. Nevertheless, *France* reflected the designs of her times as *Normandie* did hers and it would have been as inappropriate for *France* to replicate *Normandie*'s interiors, as it would have been for *Normandie* to replicate those of the *France* of 1912. Sadly, *France*, like *Normandie*, had an all-to-brief career on the Atlantic but it was economics rather than war that brought about the end to that aspect of her career. Remarkably, she was transformed into a successful Caribbean-based cruise ship for Norwegian Caribbean Cruise Line, who renamed her *Norway*. A clever choice, as it quite clearly acknowledged her owners and her new flag of registry but also seemed to be an echo of another liner from another time. With the passing of *Norway* that final link with the great and beautiful ship that was *Normandie* will be broken forever.

Normandie: she was once summed up as being: 'unrealistic, impractical, uneconomical and magnificent.' She was the pièce de résistance of all the great liners.

France, Normandie's *true successor*.

LINER OF LEGEND

BIBLIOGRAPHY

Harvey Ardman, *Normandie, Her Life and Times* (Franklin Watts, 1985)
Frank O. Braynard, *Picture History of the Normandie* (Dover, 1987)
Bruno Foucart, Charles Offrey, Francois Robichon and Claude Villiers Normandie, *Queen of the Seas* (The Vendome Press, 1985)
Arnold Kuldas, *Great Passenger Liners of the World* (Patrick Stephens, 1976)
Arnold Kludas, *Record Breakers of the North Atlantic*, Blue Riband Liners 1838-1952 (Koehlers Verlagsgesellschaft 1999)
Melvin Maddocks, *The Great Liners* (Time-Life Books, 1978)
John Maxtone-Graham, *Crossing & Cruising* (Scribners, 1992)
John Maxtone-Graham, *Liners to the Sun* (Macmillan, 1985)
John Maxtone-Graham, *The North Atlantic Run – The Only Way to Cross* (Cassell, 1972)
William H. Miller, *Passenger Liners French Style* (Carmania Press, 2001)
William H. Miller Jr, *Picture History of the French Line* (Dover, 1997)
Luis Rene Vian, *Arts Décoratifs à bord des Paquebots Français* 1800/1960 (Editions Fonmare, 1995)
Clarence Winchester, *Shipping Wonders of the World* (The Amalgamated Press Ltd, 1936)
Steamboat Bill (Journal of the Steamship Historical Society of America)

ACKNOWLEDGMENTS

My most sincere thanks must go to Christopher Hurd-Wood for the loan of many precious (and fragile) items from his collection. Without his contribution this book would not have been possible. I must also thank Campbell and Janette McCutcheon for the use of several items from their collections. I am also grateful to Tempus Publishing for giving me the opportunity to write this book.

THE NORMANDIE OF THE FRENCH LINE